SA TA NA

Thoughts are ok

Be kind to myself

Begin w a beginning mind

Don't try too hard

Stick w it

Metta - Kindness

MAITRI

Simple, Easy, Every Day Meditation™ Method

& SEED Meditation® Method

First Edition

For information write to:
McLean Meditation Institute®
411 State Route 179, Sedona, Arizona 86336

www.McLeanMeditation.com

Contents

A message from Sarah McLean

I am excited for you! You're soon to be a meditator! That means you will soon feel better, happier, and be more focused and less stressed. My goal is to make meditation so easy for you to learn and do that you'll want to incorporate it into your life immediately.

For years I have traveled around the world living, studying, and meditating in ashrams, monasteries, and temples. I've investigated and experienced many forms of meditation and have meditated for as long as eight hours a day for weeks on end. I've discovered that even when meditation is separated from its spiritual roots, it maintains its value in our modern world. And you might be happy to know that the best meditations are often the simplest ones.

Over the last 20 years I've taught thousands of people to meditate: health professionals, stay-at-home moms, retirees, CEOs, students, grandparents, Olympic and pro athletes, FBI agents, lawyers, accountants, and superior court judges, artists, and even some rock stars. Each learned to meditate because he or she knew there would be real benefits to meditation and wanted to discover for themselves how to meditate properly to release stress and create wellness and inner peace.

As I meet students in my meditation studio in Sedona, they often want me to know how truly busy their mind is – and to be assured that meditation can really work for them, too. I assure them it can.

There are so many reasons people say they can't meditate, such as: *I can't stop thinking*, or, *It's too complicated,* or, *I don't have the time*. With the Simple, Easy, Every Day Meditation™ Method people realize that whatever the reason they thought they couldn't do it wasn't a barrier to their success. I've even taught what I call *reluctant meditators*, those coerced into coming to a class by a friend or spouse. They are often the ones who have seen the greatest results!

Anyone can learn to meditate. Even if you don't have any experience or have had some "bad" meditations, don't worry.

Meditation can work for you too. If you can think a thought, *you can do it.* You don't have to change a thing – not your diet, your religion, your beliefs – nothing. You don't have to stop thinking or clear your mind; you simply must have the willingness to do it and take a short time out for it every day. You'll notice the benefits unfold naturally and effortlessly.

It's easy when you're taught correctly and have an immediate direct experience of what it feels like to do it. With the Simple, Easy, Every Day Meditation Method, known as the SEED Meditation® Method (S for *simple,* E for *easy,* E for *every*, and D for *day*), you can gain the confidence you need to continue a meditation practice that can last a lifetime.

In this book you'll find easy-to-follow instruction, research findings, and information as to how meditation releases stress, changes your brain, and transforms your life. You'll gain an understanding of why meditation works and what makes it so effective

You'll also discover that you can meditate right away, that it doesn't take superhuman powers of concentration or willpower, and, it is a truly natural process. Many students experience significant transformational benefits in many areas of their lives after only a few days with meditation.

Before beginning any new regimen, you may want to consult with your doctor, especially if you have any health conditions.

Now is a good time to ask yourself: **Why do I want to learn to meditate? What is my intention? How do I want my life to transform?**

I suggest you write your intention(s) here...

_____

_____

_____

What is Meditation?

Meditation is a word to describe the many techniques and practices, both modern and ancient, which settle your nervous system and train your brain to be more focused, engaged, and less reactive. Meditation enhances relaxation, builds vitality, and helps you to develop compassion, love, patience, generosity and forgiveness for yourself and for others.

You've probably heard of these types of meditation: mindfulness, gratitude, visualization, contemplation, walking, chanting, breath awareness, and mantra meditation. There are many, many others. The word meditation not only refers to the practices themselves, it also refers to the state of deep rest that you can experience throughout a practice.

Meditation has been around for ages. I imagine that thousands of years ago the first meditations were on fire and light – as one gazed at the sun's movement, the heavenly bodies in the night sky, or at the fire that tribes lived and worked around. Meditations probably began to include inquiry on the phenomena of life and death, sound and silence, movement and stillness, and so on. Meditation was one way for people who sought to understand the sacred and the mystical to become more intimate with the underlying creative intelligence expressed in nature.

There are many different types of meditation – some are religious, some are popular, and some you many never heard of:

- Counting or following the breath (Mindfulness, Zazen, or Vipassana)

- Repeating a mantra or word out loud or silently (Transcendental, Relaxation Response, Vedic or Mantra)

- Gazing at a sacred object or candle flame (Trataka)

- Compassion meditations (Tonglen, Metta, Loving Kindness)

- Energy center awareness (Chakra, Tantra)
- Meditation in motion (Mindfulness, Yoga, Tai Chi, Qi Gong, Walking, Kinhin, Sufi whirling)
- Native American and Indigenous people's meditation
- Gratitude, Eating, Healing, Visualizations, and various guided meditations

Here are some religious contexts for contemplative meditative practices:

Christian meditation including contemplative prayer involves being silent and praying, contemplating God, God's gifts, or scripture. Psalm 46:10 says meditation is a way of knowing God. In the bible, it is suggested to meditate on God's word.

Buddhist meditation isn't about getting closer to God; instead, it's to become intimate with one's true nature, to appreciate life, and to cultivate compassion. In addition to sitting meditation, meditation can be practiced while walking, working, chanting, and bowing.

Hindu meditation can be done while active or still, and can include prayer, ritual, and contemplation. Mostly it involves inviting the direct experience of the divine and its manifestations, or meditating on the various forms or names of God.

Islamic meditation can be performed up to five times a day in Salât, the formal way of prayer. It is not a rote prayer; instead, it's done with a mindful, meditative state. A person in Salât is instructed to meditate upon the presence of God who is watching the devotee.

Judaic meditation is a practice to still the mind. Meditations can include visualizations, prayer, and music. Some meditations are on the 72 names of God. *Hisbodedus* is a mystic practice of talking to God as you walk or sit, and expressing gratitude for your life and your gifts.

Today, meditation is practiced by millions of people worldwide. Though some who practice it may do so as an aspect of their religion, the practice itself isn't religious in nature. It's now a mainstream practice that is effectively used as an effort to reduce the effects of the increased stress of modern day life.

Whichever type of meditation you choose to do, most allow your body and brain to reach a naturally-occurring rest state. According to research, this state of rest is different than the rest you gain from sleep. According to brain wave research in meditation, while you might feel like you are sleeping in meditation, you aren't. Instead, you are deeply rested and maintaining alertness. This is why this experience found in meditation can sometimes be called the state of *restful alertness.*

Meditation is a training that helps you cultivate more present moment awareness, more focus, and a new peaceful centerpoint from which to live. It trains your attention three ways so you can more easily:

- Focus on one thing at a time,
- Attend to the present moment,
- Gain more inward focus.

You'll be more present to what is actually happening in your life instead of being distracted by doing too many things at once, or by mentally checking out. Instead of being distracted by thoughts of the future or memories of the past you'll also be more engaged in your life and can savor each moment. Though memories and desires will be a part of life, they won't replace the actual experience of the life you are living.

You'll also notice you won't be so reactive to situations, people and things, but instead, you'll be more responsive. It may even feel as if you are living a whole new normal: one where you are peaceful, creative, present, and living in real time, enjoying your life.

You'll also notice your reference point for navigating your life will change. Instead of being rocked by the outside world and its good and bad news, and navigating life in that way, you'll find a new centerpoint of peace: a calmer, more stable, perspective. This inward focus helps you to be more self-aware, so when you are not feeling centered, you'll soon realize it and know how to quickly recover and find the peace again.

After a few weeks of meditation, you will become more powerful. You will be the one in charge of where you put your attention. You'll decide what to focus on and attend to that.

It's important to remember, *knowing* about meditation will not give you these benefits; d*oing it* will.

The Simple, Easy, Every Day Meditation Method

The Simple, Easy, Every Day Meditation Method™ or SEED Meditation® Method is a simple meditation method, one that is easy to learn and practice. It's comprised of a powerful collection of practices that stem from both modern and ancient wisdom. When done daily, this method will benefit you physically, emotionally, mentally and spiritually. The practices include:

- Long, Slow, Deep Breathing Practice
- Body Awareness/Relaxation Practice
- Breath Awareness Meditation
- Heart-Centered Breath
- Self-Inquiry Practice
- A Silent Mantra Meditation

You'll also learn:

- Mindfulness Practices
- Mindful Walking Meditation
- Peacefinder Practices

Remember, in order to meditate you don't have to force your mind to be quiet; rather with regular practice, this method will help your mind to naturally settle, allowing the transcendence of thought activity so you can experience the quiet that is already there beneath the constant monologue.

You'll connect to an ever-present pure awareness which is not disturbed by thoughts of any kind.

If you turn your attention to the one who is reading this, you'll notice there is a presence there. It's what is looking through your eyes. This presence is more than just your body; it is more than just your mind: it is your very essence, what some would call your soul. It is peaceful, receptive, non-judgmental, aware, still, creative, and wise.

With meditation you will regularly connect with this aspect of you, so you can live with more "awareness of your awareness."

Everyone who learns to meditate has his or her own reason(s) and intentions for learning, and each of these reasons is like a seed.

Each time you meditate, you water that seed. The seed is nourished by the deep silence that meditation brings. Your seed's potential is unleashed to naturally grow into the fruits of your intention: awareness, freedom, inner peace, creativity, inspiration, love, present moment awareness, flexibility, stability, abundance, self-awareness, confidence, intuition, harmonious relationships, joy, creativity, fulfillment, happiness, radiance, wholeness, health, and so much more.

This collection of meditations and practices is truly all you'll need to find peace and fulfillment. Students have come back to me over the years and have told me that they continue to use this very same method and continue to experience the greatest benefits.

Meditation Misconceptions

Here are some of the many reasons people don't pursue meditation. You'll soon see why they are misconceptions:

I can't stop thinking. That's right, you can't – it is nearly impossible to stop thinking *by thinking about it.* The nature of the mind is to think, just as the nature of your eye is to see. As you develop your practice of meditation you'll find that you can easily access more and more subtle levels of thinking, and eventually, you'll experience the silence that underlies the thoughts. So even though meditation is known for "clearing your mind" it isn't done because you close your eyes and magically stop thinking. With the practices you will learn in this book, you'll find that naturally, your thought process will stop for a moment or two during meditation, again and again. Bear in mind, however, that thoughts will always be a part of your meditation, it doesn't mean you are doing it wrong. Don't try to "clear" your mind. Later in this program you'll learn why thoughts in meditation are a good thing!

I will have to work very hard to meditate correctly. No you won't. Meditation is a natural process, and you will be able to do it *effortlessly.* It does require willingness to do the practice, and the ability to sit relatively still with your eyes closed or semi-closed. And it does take a commitment to refocus your attention in meditation again and again, even when you feel like giving up. The focus for your meditation can include a sensation you feel in your body or as you breathe, it can include a visual stimulus such as a color you imagine in your mind's eye or a candle flame, or it can be something you hear - a sound of a bell, or a thought you think. Whatever your focus you choose, you'll need to spend a few minutes every day to turning your attention gently toward it. Anyone can meditate, and most people can do it easily the very first time.

I am so busy; I don't have the time for this. How long do you wait in line for a latte? How much time do you spend checking your email or surfing the web? Most of us can find five minutes each day to meditate. And five minutes of meditation is better than none at all. Think of meditation as the perfect way to reduce stress and to rejuvenate your mind and body. It's like a mini-nap. It's totally worth taking this time out for a time in. If you meditate for a short time each day you'll receive more benefits than sitting in front of the TV. It's all about priorities, and your health and happiness are probably a priority for you.

My knees don't bend like that. The lotus position, a traditional yoga posture for meditation, is not required for a successful meditation. If sitting Indian style or crossing your legs is uncomfortable, don't do it. You'll be more distracted and this may keep you from being able to settle down in your meditation. Be comfortable. Most people prefer to sit in a chair with their back supported. Some, who can, sit on a cushion on the floor. Bear in mind it is best not to lie down (you'll fall asleep and that is NOT meditation.) You can meditate while you are sitting almost anywhere – as long as you are not driving. There are even standing and walking meditations. You'll learn about those later.

Meditation will make me too relaxed to be competitive. Most people are used to functioning while being tense or stressed, and they feel being hyped up is the only way to get motivated – using Red Bull, caffeine, sugar and a competitive outlook, beating themselves up until they get it right. In reality, over time, the effects of stress can lessen your ability to concentrate or make good decisions. With meditation, you won't become lazy or too relaxed; instead, you'll be clearer, more creative, and better able to respond. You'll gain focus, creativity, and better concentration. You'll and live your life from a place of centeredness and balance, establishing a "new normal." You'll learn you can *do less and accomplish more.*

The goal of meditation is to have mystic visions and revelations. In Sedona where I live and work, there can be an emphasis on having mystical experiences both in and out of meditation. Though spiritual insights can occur, they aren't as prevalent in meditation as one might think. What I have noticed in my over 20 years of meditating is that meditation helps to remove the veil of stress that can often shroud one's perception of themselves and others. Meditation does seem to increase appreciation for the wonder of life and can enhance a feeling of connectedness and inner knowing. With a regular practice of meditation, some notice increased synchronicities, enhanced intuition, and an expanded awareness of the divine. People can find that in meditation they lose track of time and space, and no longer sense where their body begins and ends. This is not about connecting to another world, instead, it's about connecting to your own awareness. Meditation facilitates a deep connection with who you really are, and how you express yourself in this world.

I'll have to change my religion. Many mediation techniques originate from Eastern religions and philosophies, but the practice of modern day meditation doesn't depend on either. Regardless of your background or beliefs you can meditate. Meditation may make you more connected with God or your own inner world. This is true for anyone whether atheist, Christian, Muslim, Jewish, Quaker, Buddhist, Hindu, or Jain. Meditation is a personal practice, not a religion. It's about closing your eyes, sitting still, and reconnecting with who you really are in the present moment. It helps to reduce stress, enhance wellbeing, and increase your self-awareness. I'm religious about my meditation practice.

I'll have to wear different clothing. You don't need to wear a special robe, hat, or love beads. . What you wear doesn't make you more of a meditator. Meditation is a personal experience; you do it the way you want to – sit where you'd like, wear what you'd like and simply follow the techniques that suit you and your lifestyle. Just because some people may insist that those who are *really* into meditation should look or live a certain way, it's best to heed your own inner wisdom, trust yourself, and do what you want. Stay with your own integrity.

It is for weirdoes. I'm sure I used to be considered weird by my friends and family as they got married, had kids, got serious jobs, and eventually became really stressed. Now that their kids are in their teens, they realize that I might've been onto something. I chose to make meditation a priority and headed off to an ashram, lived in a monastery, and pursued this path. Now they ask me how to be happy and peaceful. I'm not weird anymore. That being said, some people who meditate are definitely weird and have really unusual beliefs. But there are people like that everywhere.

What Does Meditation Require?

Three ingredients are required to practice any meditation technique:

1. Your willingness to do the practice,

2. Your non-judgmental attention,

3. An object to focus on.

Your Willingness: Though quieting the mind's activity and meditation in general can seem impossible and can be frustrating, it's best if you approach meditation with a commitment to stick with it. I'm not only referring to continuing your meditation practice daily, I am also suggesting sticking with the meditation practice throughout the entire meditation period. Whether you are meditating for 5 or 25 minutes, don't quit in the middle of your meditation period even if you have a strong impulse to do something else. When you stay with the practice in the midst of the urge to react or do something else, you'll change your relationship to your thoughts and even tame the reactive mind. Meditation is about training your brain, or retraining it to be less impulsive or compulsive. Be willing to finish an entire meditation period.

Your Attention: Rather than an intense, judgmental focus, you will use an easy, open focus - a gentle attention. It's simple. Here's an exercise to experience the ease of focus:

For a minute, turn your attention to your breath. Notice the way it naturally moves in and out of your body, notice how it sounds, and how the body expands and contracts with each inhale and exhale.

Okay, now shift your attention to your right hand. You don't have to move it or look at it, simply focus your attention on it. Feel it. Now, switch your focus to your left hand. Now, switch back to the right.

Was that easy? I imagine it was. That's the ease of attention that you'll use in meditation. And the ease of refocusing, which is necessary, even for the most experienced meditator. Yes, it is natural to get distracted and have your mind drift off to other things. However, once you notice your attention is no longer on the focus of your meditation, all you need to do is simply refocus. Don't judge yourself or give up. It doesn't matter how many times you have to refocus. Later, you'll read about why thoughts arise and disrupt your attention.

A Focus: The focus of most meditations is often something simple – it could be a sound, sensation, or something you see. The sensation could be the feel of your breath as you breathe, or the sensations of your body as it moves. You could focus on a sound – whether you make it, hear it, or even think it (most thoughts are words you say or hear in your mind). Or, you could focus on something you see, be it an image that you visualize in your mind's eye, or a real object you gaze at such as a star, a candle flame, a geometric pattern, or a picture of a saint.

Though you can focus on something you **taste**, as in a mindful eating exercise, it isn't prudent to use taste as a focus for every day meditation. The sense of **smell** is also not a good focus for your meditation. Though aromas can create a mood or a memory that supports your meditation practice, as incense or aromatic oils do, scents and aromas tend to fade from your awareness in only a short period of time, so are not ideal to use as a focus for meditation.

The Five Essentials of Meditation

Here are five essentials for a successful meditation practice:

(1) it's okay to have thoughts during meditation, (2) don't try too hard, (3) let go of expectations, (4) be kind to yourself, and (5) stick with it.

1. It's Okay to Have Thoughts

If you're thinking, "I probably can't meditate because I have too many thoughts," then you are not alone. Perhaps you've already tried to meditate for a few minutes once or twice, and it "didn't work." You sat down, closed your eyes, and tried to clear your mind but couldn't. Then you gave up.

Students in my classes often tell me, "I can't stop thinking." My reply is, "That's right, you can't stop the thoughts." I explain that you can't stop thoughts by thinking about not thinking – because the nature of the mind is to think, just as the nature of your eyes is to see. If you try to stop thinking, your effort will make you frustrated and possibly give you a headache.

So even though meditation will help to quiet your mind, it's not because you completely stop thinking during the practice. Instead, the meditation practices you will learn help to naturally settle your mind and body, allowing you to access more subtler levels of thoughts and impulses. Sometimes the thought processes may even stop for a moment or two.

However, bear in mind, this stillness of mind is not created by somehow magically stopping your thoughts, instead, it's a natural settling down process that occurs when you meditate properly. And over time, as you interrupt the constant flow of thoughts, you become more familiar with the silence that is always present underlying the thoughts– what I call the silence of your soul. The stillness of the mind is revealed through meditating. Later, you'll learn that thoughts, colors, ideas, emotions, and physical activity in meditation are often an indication that you are releasing stress, and that's a good thing.

2. Don't Try Too Hard

I once taught meditation to a heart surgeon and his wife on New Year's Day (he had called and set up an appointment at 9 a.m., wanting to start the year off right.) After they learned to meditate he asked how he could "get good at it." I responded by asking him how he got to be "good" at surgery. Practice, *right*? Well, it's the same with meditation.

At first, you may try to do it "right." You can't *try* to do anything without the mind getting involved, so you'll soon find that trying, forcing, or concentrating creates more thoughts and bad habits. Instead of expending mental effort or attempting to have a certain experience, such as a quiet mind, you'll discover that your attention your mind and body will naturally settle down when you do the practices outlined in this book.

As with any natural experience, too much effort can ruin the process. For example, *trying* to go to sleep, even if you're tired, can make you miserable. *Trying* to come up with a new idea and force your way through a creative block is the same—it rarely works. *Trying* to meditate is similar, because meditation is a natural settling down of the body and mind, a relatively effortless pursuit.

Remember, you don't get "good" at meditating by trying hard, instead, you'll learn to use a gentle easy focus and refocus again and again. The only effort required is the effort to set aside the time and space for your regular practice. Some of us are in the habit of having to be doing something in order to feel satisfied, and that includes "doing" meditation, or trying hard at it. Instead, meditation trains you be gentle with yourself and allowing the natural experience to happen.

3. Let Go of Expectations

You may have preconceived notions of what is supposed to be going on during meditation – how you should feel or what you should experience. Many of us have seen pictures of the monks in robes or yogis sitting cross-legged. Some of us have heard stories about the wild experiences some meditators have.

I love to teach those who have no expectations about meditation. First timers come and sit with me for 15-20 minutes and then report that they felt great and that it was easy. I attribute this to "beginner's mind," an open mind, a mind free from expectations, labels, and judgments. It's important to treat each meditation as innocently as the first time you learned. During meditation, you'll have all kinds of experiences—some you'll like better than others, and some you'll want to repeat in your next meditation. Instead of waiting for something to happen, let go of expectations or wanting your meditation to go a certain way. Allow your body and mind to naturally eliminate stress and allow the natural nourishing effect to unfold.

I'm often asked, "How will I know I'm doing it right?" My answer is that when you approach meditation without expectations and with ease, welcoming whatever experiences arise, then you are doing it right. Avoid trying too hard and avoid controlling your experience. Instead of judging your meditations as good or bad based on the experiences you have in meditation, trust the process. You'll see if the meditation is working and if you are doing it right by seeing the changes in your life. You will find you are happier, more relaxed, less stressed, more creative, more perceptive, and more appreciative.

4. Be Kind to Yourself

An essential key to meditating correctly is being kind to yourself. This is one of the most important things I've learned through my years of practicing and teaching meditation. While it should go without saying, I still say it because many people have learned to be tough on themselves in order to achieve their goals. Being tough on yourself does not help change your behavior; it's simply a bad habit. Instead, be gentle towards yourself as you commit to transforming your life. Don't get down on yourself in meditation if your mind wanders, or you get bored, or the experiences you have in meditation don't fulfill your expectations. Don't compare your experience to others'. Be nice to yourself when you are not meditating too.

5. Stick with It

Finally, meditation only works if you stick with it and don't give up. During your meditation period your mind may wander, you may feel restless, have a brilliant idea, or think of something you simply must do (like check your email or write something down) and you may want to give up or stop right then. But don't! Instead, begin again by gently returning your awareness to the focus of your meditation. I call this momentary awareness of being lost in thought the "choice point." It's at this point that you have to make the choice whether to continue your meditation, or to give up, or to go on with your plans and daydreams. Make the choice to keep meditating! Have the discipline to do the practices and stick with the entire meditation period you have committed to each day, whether it's five minutes or half an hour, even if you're antsy or bored.

By staying with the practice, you will create a new relationship with your reactive mind. As you let the thoughts and impulses come and go without taking action, you change your relationship to your mind, and shift toward witnessing your mental activity rather than being at its mercy. This will lead you to a deeper understanding of how your mind works.

Often when you feel fidgety or frustrated in meditation it's an indication that you're releasing a lot of stress. If you stick with the practice, the stress will dissipate and you'll experience a "meditator's high". Don't quit before the bliss! Don't quit the program either.

Stay with it each day. Meditating every day will give you the benefits, but not meditating won't. To get the most benefit out of your meditation, **it's ideal is to meditate 15- 30 minutes twice a day.** If you can't do that, once a day will give you some benefit. Even five minutes once a day is better than not meditating at all.

Even if you don't think anything is happening in meditation, science shows dramatic changes occur in the minds and bodies of consistent meditators. And the changes occur long after the meditation period is over. You'll soon believe it once you see the benefits for yourself.

The Basics

Find a comfortable place to meditate. The ideal place to meditate will be a quiet place indoors. Even though it seems romantic to meditate on a mountaintop somewhere it isn't practical for most people. Designate an area in your home or office where you'll be able to do your meditation practices regularly, perhaps in your bedroom sitting up on your bed with your back against the headboard, or in a chair or on your favorite cushion in a room that's not cluttered. Once you've found your spot, you might want to make it special with flowers, pictures of friends and loved ones, lighting a candle, or placing meaningful objects there.

If you can't find the perfect spot, don't let that be a barrier to your meditation. I meditate on planes, in doctor's offices, and in my car (obviously not when I am driving) or any place I can find some alone time. I'm often in the grocery store parking lot with eyes closed meditating between appointments. You can meditate almost anywhere you feel safe and will be undisturbed.

Keep distractions to a minimum. Wherever you choose to meditate, do whatever you can to limit distractions. Turn off the ringer on your phone and turn off your TV, iPod, CD player, and the sound off your computer. Do not listen to music while meditating, even if it is called "meditation music." Music can tend to charm your attention outwardly. In meditation, you train your attention on the inner world, not on the world out there. Put a "do not disturb" sign on your door and ask your friends, partner, or family not to bother you during this time. Leave your animals outside or in another room.

If you do get interrupted in the middle of your meditation, go back and meditate for at least five more minutes to release any stress that was created. And definitely finish your meditation period with a few minutes of sitting still.

Find something to sit on. Now that you have a good place and time, find something to sit on. The main thing is to be comfortable. Many people choose to sit in a chair. Sit with your feet flat on the ground and your back upright, chin in.

If you decide to sit on the floor, make sure that your rear is lifted off the ground a little – use a cushion or *zafu* (a round Japanese-style cushion) or fold a pillow in half to help you to keep your back straight. This considered very important in meditation. You might sit "Indian-style" or with one leg folded in front of the other on the floor. Don't try to fold your legs around in a complicated position unless it's really comfortable.

I often sit up against the headboard of my bed for my morning meditation, though sometimes it seems like I am still in the 'sleep' mode, I am getting a restful alertness experience through a short period of meditation before I get up and go!

However you sit you'll have to figure out what to do with your hands. You can clasp them together and let them rest in your lap or try a meditation mudra. Whichever position you choose, rest your hands lightly in your lap or on your knees or on the arms of the chair. Your head can tilt down very slightly, chin in. Aim to sit relatively still and in comfort. You can close your eyes, or leave them capped. Capped means that your eyes are just barely open, gazing toward the ground at a point about 3 feet in front of you. If you sit with your eyes closed, you can open them if you feel anxious, but shut them again right away.

Do not lie down when you meditate. I know you want to, but don't. Yes it is relaxing, but if you think about it, you've trained yourself for years to fall asleep lying down. Even if you don't think you will, believe me, you will fall asleep when you meditate lying down. Then the whole process becomes one of a sleeping meditation, or napping, which is a different thing altogether. You can lie down before or after you meditate for a few minutes. That might satisfy your desire to get horizontal. The only exception is if you have to lie down because of a medical condition.

Find a time that works for you to meditate. Although there are recommend specific times in the day for meditation, the most important thing is to find a time that works for you and make it a habit. Set yourself up to succeed. Schedule it just as you would any other important meeting. Let people know not to disturb you. You really can meditate almost any time, and almost anywhere if you sit relatively still with your eyes closed. However, here are the recommended times:

The first meditation ideally should be in the early morning. Get the meditation in before the day gets going. This way you'll be sure to get it in before you do anything else and get distracted. Eat after you meditate. Sleep is one way your body reduces stress, so this often makes any early morning meditation the most settled meditation of the day. At Deepak Chopra's center they say *RPM* (rise, pee, meditate.)

The second meditation should be in the evening between work and dinner. It's a great transition period. I call this the *Happy Hour* meditation. Whatever you do when you get home from work, whether it's pour a glass of wine, surf the internet, or flipping on the TV, make time to meditate first.

If you can't meditate either before breakfast or before dinner, the next best time is before lunch. Though meditation may relax you and is proven to improve sleep, it isn't because it's to be done just before bed. Instead, it's because it releases enough stress so you can sleep soundly later on. Meditation in general can increase or stabilize your physical energy and quite possibly could interrupt your sleep if you do it too close to bedtime. If you must meditate late in the evening, choose to start it at least three hours before bedtime, and an hour after you eat.

Don't meditate on a full stomach. It's best not to eat too much before you meditate because digestion seems to activate the body and the mind. If you do have to eat before you meditate, try to wait at least an hour to meditate. You can meditate before breakfast, before lunch or before dinner… easy.

Find an easy way to time it! To monitor the meditation period, you can use the vibrate mode of your cell phone's alarm (turn the ringer off), or peek at your watch or a clock from time to time. Use one of the many apps for your phone. Don't use an alarm or timer that you have to get up to turn off. Make sure you stick to the allotted time, no matter what your mind says.

Stick to it. Whatever length of time you have determined you'll meditate for, stick to it once you start. Whether it's 10 minutes 20 minutes 30 minutes... don't change your time commitment in the middle of your meditation because you suddenly feel restless and bored, or have the thought, "This isn't working" or "I have too many emails to just sit here." Thoughts are a part of meditation, do not struggle against them. A restless meditation is a good meditation, even if it doesn't 'feel' that way, because stress is being released.

When you make a commitment to sit through these rough spots, you'll have released a great amount of stress and will feel really refreshed after the meditation. You'll also change your relationship to that reactive part of your brain. You'll become more responsive. That's why committing to a time keeps the mind a little more settled, and trains the brain and body to meditate.

Take your time coming out of it. To end your meditation, sit for 2 – 3 minutes after you stop the practice with your eyes closed. It's called the Integration Period. Give yourself this time. It is very important. You may want to jump up right away but don't. Even if it doesn't feel that way, when you meditate, you reach a very deep state of rest; it's actually another state of consciousness sometimes called *restful awareness*. Your nervous system can be rested as in sleep, and jumping up in the middle of the rest can create a jolt to the nervous system, causing more stress. The 2 – 3 minute rest period after a meditation is an important time to integrate the silence into your daily activity. You can even lie down during that time.

Make it a priority. Ideally, meditation is something that you'll work into your daily routine – like brushing your teeth or taking a shower. Even though it sometimes isn't fun, or exciting, meditation will definitely make your day, and then your life, better. You don't have to commit to meditating twice a day every day for the rest of your life, but you could aim for something – say 20 minutes at least once a day – this will bring about noticeable changes in your life. It is said that it takes three weeks to create a habit. Make sure that your goal is reasonable, and give it a chance. The benefits unfold naturally if you keep with it.

Hand Positions in Meditation

Hand positions, or hand *mudras,* have been around since ancient times and are often depicted in statues and paintings. Though most people sit with their hands folded in their lap, images of meditators often show hand positions that may seem unfamiliar to you.

Mudras are hand, body, and eye postures used to invoke certain energy patterns and states of consciousness. Specifically, hand mudras are considered to prevent the dissipation of subtle life energy by keeping energy channels connected. These connections allow subtle energy or prana to channel along pathways to affect the mind and body. Their effects are very subtle and can be sensed by those with refined awareness.

Gyan or Jnana Mudra – the mudra of knowledge and wisdom:

Connect the thumb and the forefinger (tip to tip, not tip to nail) the other fingers are straight but relaxed. Keep the pressure between the thumb and forefinger light. Lay your hands on your knees palms up for connecting to the heavens, or palms down for grounding. This is the traditional hand posture for meditations originating from the Hindu tradition though it is seen in artistic depictions of Jesus Christ and Buddha.

Dhyana or Cosmic Mudra: The mudra of meditation concentration:

Lay the right hand over left (some prefer the other way around) with the thumb tips slightly meeting. The index finger and thumbs form an oval. If you bring your attention to your hands in meditation and find that you are pressing your thumbs together forcefully, that's a sign that you need to relax. If you realize your hands have gone slack and your thumbs are no longer touching, that's a sign that need to adjust your posture and increase your awareness. This is the traditional hand posture for Buddhist meditations.

Namaste or Anjali Mudra: The mudra of respect for another and adoration of the Divine:

Palms of the hands are pressed together gently. All fingers are together and pointing straight up. They can be placed in front of the heart or at the forehead (between the eyebrows.) This is a traditional mudra for praying and greeting each other in respect in Hinduism, Buddhism, and other cultures which essentially means, "I honor the place in you in which the Divine dwells, which is the same as in me. Namaste." Pronounced nah-mas-stay.

Mindfulness

Every meditation begins with mindfulness. The term *mindfulness* refers to the practice of bringing your attention into the present moment and the present activity, and filling your mind with the actual experience. You engage your senses and your awareness, maintaining a nonjudgmental attitude while you pay attention to what you are doing, while you are doing it. If you get distracted, as in meditation, you simply notice the mind's usual commentary and refocus.

Mindfulness can be practiced formally as a seated meditation, or informally while in activity, in almost any situation.

Mindfulness is a good way to start any meditation. Start with where you are, mindfully, and go from there.

When practiced formally it involves sitting down and paying attention to the activity of your thoughts, your body sensations, and movement and sound of your breath. This focus settles the body and mind and you begin to experience the silent backdrop behind all activity.

Any activity you perform regularly can become a mindful or meditative practice including eating, driving, washing, cleaning the house, and, of course, walking. Mindfulness ultimately becomes a way of life as you move from the domain of "doing" to "being" while you perform action.

You can be mindful of the sensations in your feet while walking, or of the feeling of warm soapy water on your hands as you do the dishes. Or the sound of the water. You can eat mindfully too. As you sit down to eat you can completely engage in the process of eating, without judgment. Notice the way your body is positioned, the sensations that arise in your body, and the mind's responses to those sensations. Note what you see, smell, taste, feel, and hear as engage in drinking or biting, chewing and swallowing.

When you notice the mind wandering, simply bring your attention back to the process of eating, what is actually occurring, rather than your thoughts about what you are doing. Mindfulness is a continual refocusing on the present moment.

Mindfulness practices, along with meditation, train your attention, and bring your awareness back (i.e. from the past or the future or distraction of any kind) into the present moment, and to what is happening while it's happening.

You will stay focused and engaged in the actual experience of your life. This is vital, as many of us only have ideas about what is happening rather than being truly present for the direct experience of life.

This moment is the only real thing. Tomorrow, or the next moment, will be experienced in what we call the here and now. When? Now? The present moment, the one right now, is where and when your life is lived. Mindfulness practices will help you to be here, now.

Long, Slow, Deep Breathing Practice

In ancient times, breathing exercises were practiced before a period of meditation to settle down the mind. They are known as the practice of pranayama – a Sanskrit word derived from the root word *prana,* which means breath or life force, and *ayama* which means expansion. This simple practice of Long, Slow, Deep Breathing is the perfect complement to a Sitting Meditation. It naturally relaxes you and slows you down, though can give you a natural energy boost. The rhythm of your breath often reflects the activity of the body and mind.

When stressed, your breath becomes rapid shallow, or you hold your breath or even forget to breathe at all. When you give yourself long, slow, deep breaths through your nose, it sends a signal to your mind and body to shift into the parasympathetic response. Researchers found slow, deep breathing to be as effective in reducing anxiety as antidepressants. It enhances your self-awareness, helps you to regain peace when stressed, and is a great way to get a natural lift, especially in the middle of the day. Blood circulation in the diaphragm increases stimulates and enlivens the entire body–which is why it's best not to do this practice too close to bedtime. Before you begin, you may want to consult your doctor to be sure it's right for you. It is suggested to do this exercise for 3 – 10 minutes before the Sitting Meditation.

Here's how:

- Find a way to time yourself. Sit in a comfortable position.

- You can keep your eyes open, but you might want to close or cap your eyes. Capping is a practice of maintaining a soft unfocused gaze directed two to three feet in front of you and helps integrate silence into activity.

- Rest your hands comfortably in your lap.

- Give yourself a few moments to relax your body from head to toe. Soften your belly.

- Inhale slowly through the nostrils, fill your abdominal area first, then the chest cavity, then the clavicle area. Visualize expanding your body in 360 degrees as you inhale.

- Once the lungs are completely filled, hold the breath only for a few seconds while pressing the shoulders back and expand the chest out, so the pressure of the breath on the diaphragm can be felt.

- Exhale slowly through the nostrils beginning with the clavicle area, then the chest cavity, and then the abdominal area, contracting your navel toward your spine to clear your lungs completely. Hold the breath out for a few seconds.

- Never force an exhale or inhale.

- As you your muscles in your belly, chest, and shoulders you begin to feel the sensation of a natural bellows-like motion in the diaphragm.

- Continue with your long, slow, deep breath, keeping the length of the inhale and exhale equal. For example, if your inhale takes 4 seconds...exhale for 4 seconds. Keep the length of the hold between inhales and exhales equal, pausing for a count or two. You may average 5–9 full breaths per minute.

Meditation Practices

MEDITATION USING THE SENSE OF TOUCH

Meditations on the sensation of touch can include those done sitting still or while you move. When you use touch in meditation, you're not actually reaching out to feel something outside of yourself. You simply feel the subtle sensations in your body, breath, or movement.

Some people focus on the subtle sense of touch as they feel their body from the inside out – scanning their body with their awareness or bringing their attention to the sensation of pain or tension in the body. Some people focus on an emotion they want to cultivate, such as a feeling of gratitude or love. These also use the subtle sense of touch.

Meditations using the sense of touch can also include movement. You simply *feel* your body as you move through your environment in time and space. Or you can meditate on the sense of touch while being massaged and bring your attention to the sensations as the body is touched.

Some meditations combine what you feel with what you see – as in imagining breathing in light or color as you relax different areas of the body. Others combine touch and sound, as in feeling your breath and using a mantra. Some can involve a string of beads you measure one by one with your fingers and combining touch with using the sense of sound – repeating a mantra or prayer either silently or out loud while sitting, or walking. This practice is used by Hindus (called *japa*) as they chant, by Catholics as they pray (the Rosary), in the Greek and Islamic traditions as they pray, and in the Tibetan Buddhist tradition as they walk, chant and measure beads.

Moving meditations can be helpful to those who find it difficult to sit still. They can include spontaneous and free-form movements or highly structured, choreographed, repetitive patterns such as:

- **Yoga.** In the Western world, yoga involves a series of postures that integrate your breath, attention and movement.

- **Tai chi or Qi gong.** Both of these techniques are said to move the life force energy sometimes call *prana, qi, ki* or *chi.* Tai chi involves gentle, deliberate circular movements combined with deep breathing. Qi gong arises from ancient China and integrates physical postures, breathing techniques and focused attention.

- **Sufi dancing:** Developed in medieval Islam, practitioners walk or dance in a rhythmic fashion while silent or chanting. The intent is to focus the mind on a specific quality of the divine. You can whirl too for a time, as some whirling dervishes do, and notice how the stillness can be found within activity.

The meditation practices and exercises you'll learn in this program that focus on "feeling" and "touch" are:

- Body Awareness/Relaxation Practice

- Breath Awareness Meditation

- Heart-Centered Breath

- Mindful Walking Meditation

Body Awareness/Relaxation Technique

This Body Awareness practice will help you be more present to how your body feels and ultimately, this leads to more self-awareness. Once you enjoy the body as it relaxes, you can be more attuned to its signals of comfort and discomfort throughout the day. As you do this exercise, adopt the attitude of an explorer: feel, watch, listen, and detect sensations as they come and go. As you explore, you become the witness of your body and breath, and this helps you develop present-moment awareness.

Read through the following instructions. Review them again each day before you practice. It's natural not to remember each and every step, but as time goes by it will become second nature. Practice this Body Awareness technique for 10 minutes. You can do it by itself, or use it prior to engaging in a silent Mantra Meditation or Breath Awareness Meditation.

Here's how:

- Do this practice with your eyes open, half-closed, or closed.

- Sit up comfortably.

- Let your breath remain natural, breathing through your nose. It might slow down, speed up, get deeper or shallower, or stop for a moment. Feel it, and let it be as it is.

- Move your awareness slowly, deliberately, from your head to your toes, in a continuous flow.

- Feel your body from the inside out, noticing every sensation.

- As you focus on each body part in a continuous fashion, relax each area and any tension you find.

- Feel and relax your head (including scalp, forehead, ears, eyes, cheeks, mouth, tongue, chin, and jaw),

- Relax your neck, shoulders,

- Relax your right arm, hand and fingers,

- Relax your left arm, hand, and fingers.

- Relax your upper back, upper chest and diaphragm,

- Relax your upper, mid, and lower back.

- Relax your belly, hips, pelvis, rear.

- Relax your right leg from hip to toes.

- Relax your left leg from hip to toes.

- Notice how you are being supported by the chair or cushion.

- Scan your body a second time from head to toes. As you do this second round, let your attention rest on areas of your body that you normally would disapprove of, avoid, or areas where you find pain, discomfort, or illness.

- Investigate all areas of your body with your awareness, even places you would normally skip over like your earlobes, knuckles, and back of your knees. Do this with a non-judgmental attitude, as you explore the sensations.

• If you have an area of illness, or dis-ease, you may notice that you want it to change or heal. Perhaps you send light to it, or wish it were different. Instead of *thinking about doing something*, gently return your attention to the area you are focused on and *simply feel the actual sensations of that area from the inside out*; do not try to heal or change it with your mind or your will. Your attention will make the change on its own.

• As you experience sensations in your body, you may find you begin to tell yourself a story about a specific area such as, *My knees hurt*, or *My stomach is too big*, or *I am too tired to do this*. Once you realize that you're storytelling, gently return your attention to the area you are focused on and simply feel the sensations of that area from the inside out; do not focus on the thought about it. Being present with the pain or discomfort without trying to change it is called "bearing witness."

• Feel free to pause and refocus your attention from the story or thought to the physical sensation as many times as it takes. Be patient and kind to yourself. Don't judge your experience or worry about how many times your attention drifts away from the body.

• Feel and "be with" any sensations, even discomfort, rather avoid the sensations, or attempting to make the sensations go away, change them, or create a story. You may be accustomed to avoiding certain areas, so this exercise is the opportunity to allow yourself to experience whatever sensation is actually present with curiosity and nonjudgmental awareness.

• Welcome whatever you feel, or if you don't have much sensation at all, welcome that, too. When thoughts about the future or past distract you from your focus, or you see colors, faces, or places, in your mind's eye, simply notice them, then simply return your focus to your body's sensations.

• Continue this practice for the predetermined period of time. When you're finished, take your attention off your body. Notice your state of mind as you sit still for another few minutes.

- After a few minutes, slowly open your eyes (if they were closed), and take your time moving back into activity. Or, if you prefer, you can begin a silent sitting meditation such as the *Breath Awareness Meditation* or *Mantra Meditation* that follow.

Breath Awareness Meditation

Sometimes called mindfulness meditation, Insight, Zazen, or Vipassana, this simple, non-religious breath-awareness practice can be done anywhere, anytime. It is used by people around the world.

Breath is the essence of life. You inhale for the first time as you arrive in the world, and from that moment on, you take approximately 17,000 breaths each day, which over a lifetime totals about 500 million. Paying attention to the breath is a simple way to connect to the present moment and become more self-aware and more mindful. Meditating on your breath involves bringing your focus to the subtle sensation of the process of inhaling and exhaling. Some practices involve counting the breaths you 'feel'.

Read through the following instructions. Review them again before your practice. It's natural not to remember each and every step, but as time goes by it will become second nature.

Here's how:

- Determine how long you'll be doing this practice before you start. It can be about 5 - 20 minutes.

- Keep track of the time by looking at a clock or watch. Don't set an alarm that will make you get up to shut it off.

- Sit comfortably. Your eyes can be open, half-closed, or closed. Turn off music, sounds, TVs, what have you.

- Remember to let go of expectations, be kind to yourself, complete the entire practice period, and don't give up.

- Breathe naturally through your nose.

- Bring your awareness to each breath, focusing on the movement and sensations the air creates as it moves in and out of your body.

- As the breath enters and leaves through your nostrils, notice the cool air on the inhale, the warmer air on the exhale.

- Feel your chest and back rise and fall on the inhalation and exhalation.

- Feel your belly expand and contract.

- This isn't about imagining or controlling the breath, but simply feeling its sensations.

- Allow the breath to come and go in its own natural pattern. There's nothing to figure out, nothing to control, nothing to change.

- Keep your focus on each breath. Then, for a few breaths, let your attention rest on the natural pause between the exhale and inhale.

- Whenever you notice your attention has drifted away from your breath—shifting to a noise, to a thought, or to some other distraction—simply refocus your attention to the breath.

- This is a practice, so don't give yourself a hard time about losing focus. Distractions are natural. Be kind to yourself without concern for how many times you drift off.

- If you get distracted by a physical sensation, recognize it, but don't attempt to figure out why it's happening, or go into a story about it. Simply keep the sensation company with your awareness. When it dissipates, gently return your attention to your breath.

- You may find your breathing spontaneously gets faster or slower, deeper or shallower; it may even pause for a moment. Observe any changes without controlling, resisting, anticipating, or expecting anything. Don't judge your experience or worry about how many times your attention drifts away.

- Rest your attention on the breath and its sensations for your predetermined period of time.

- When the period comes to an end, take your attention off your breath.

- Sit or lie still for a few minutes more. This is the *Integration Period.* After a few minutes, slowly open your eyes and take your time moving back into activity

Heart-Centered Breath

Your heart does much more than pump blood through your veins . . . it is wise. It informs your body and mind with its intelligence and wisdom. There are as many neurons in the heart as in some sections of the brain; in fact, the heart's magnetic field is actually stronger than the brain's—5,000 times more!

When you pay attention to your heart, by feeling the heart beat or simply by dropping your attention to the area behind your breastbone, you enliven its intelligence and its qualities of peace, love, compassion, joy, gratitude, and inclusiveness. The heart sends signals to the brain that change the entire nervous system, reducing stress hormones, enhancing your immune system, and increasing anti-aging hormones.

The Heart-Centered Breath can be used anytime: while meditating, walking, or while listening to someone. It can be practiced for 2 – 10 minutes either by itself, or as a prelude to Breath Awareness and Silent Mantra Meditation practices.

Here's how:

- Get into a comfortable seated position. Settle down. Your eyes can be open, capped, or closed. Scan and relax your body.

- Bring your attention to your breath as you breathe through your nose. Don't try to control or regulate your breath or its rhythm. Feel the sensations of the inhale and exhale of your breath, the coolness of your breath on the inhale, the warmth on the exhale.

- Let your body naturally settle. After a moment or two, bring your attention to the rise and fall of your chest. Imagine looking inward toward your heart. Let your attention rest there for a breath or two.

- Next, imagine your breath is moving into and out of your heart center as if it were a doorway to your breath. (You can place your hand over the center of your chest, on your breastbone, to help to keep your attention focused there.)

- Match the length of the inhale to the length of the exhale. Breathe in this rhythmic way for three or four full breaths.

- Now return your attention to the natural breath pattern without controlling the rhythm, depth, or speed. Continue imagining the breath moving in front of you—in and out of the center of your chest.

- Continue like this for 2 – 10 minutes, refocusing the attention on your breath when you notice it has shifted to something else. Be kind to yourself.

- When you are finished, sit silently for a few moments with your eyes closed before engaging back into any activity.

Mindful Walking Meditation

Walking meditation, called *kinhin* in Zen Buddhism, is a moving meditation practice originating from the Buddhist tradition. Walking meditations help the body to remain at ease and to recover from any tension that builds up due to long periods of sitting. While it cultivates mindfulness and increased awareness, it can also be a lot of fun and lowers stress.

This Walking Meditation can be done anywhere: in a tranquil forest, in a park, on a city sidewalk, up and down a hallway or around a room. You can walk in a circle or a line going back and forth, inside or out of doors. Some people use the practice as they walk a labyrinth.

As you walk, you simply attend to your senses: feeling the earth beneath the feet, the movement of your body, the ever-changing balance of the body, the sounds you hear, what you see, etc. This practice can help you become intimate with the body in action – and for some this creates a more observable focus than a still meditation.

After some practice, you'll learn to use it anytime: you can use it informally when you go shopping, at work, or walking to or from your car. You can learn to enjoy walking for its own sake – instead of the usual planning and thinking that can distract you. You learn to be where you are, in the present moment, as you move through your life.

Read through the following instructions. Do this meditation for a fixed period of time as you would a sitting meditation, it's suggested to do this technique for 10-20 minutes. You can do it by itself, or after or before a Silent Mantra or Breath Awareness Meditation.

Here's how:

- Turn off your cell phone, even the vibrate mode. Do this practice in silence.

- Select a quiet place where you can walk comfortably.

- Begin by standing at one end of this "walking path," with your feet firmly planted on the ground.

- Let your hands rest easily, wherever they are comfortable. Close your eyes for a moment, center yourself, and feel your body standing on the earth. Give yourself a deep breath in and out.

- Keep your eyes lowered, gazing toward the ground a few steps ahead.

- While walking, attend to the sensation of your feet, noticing the contact as it touches the ground. Feel the pressure on the bottoms of your feet and the other natural sensations of standing.

- If your attention drifts away, notice what else took your attention and then return to the feet.

- Begin to walk slowly. Let yourself walk with a sense of ease and awareness. Pay attention to your body as you go from being still to movement.

- With each step feel the sensations of lifting your foot and leg off of the earth. Be aware as you place each foot on the earth.

- Relax and let your walking be easy and natural and mindful.

- When you come to the end of your path, pause for a moment. Center yourself, mindfully turn around, and pause again so that you can be aware of the first step as you walk back.

- You can experiment with the speed, walking at whatever pace keeps you most present.

- Continue to walk for ten or twenty minutes or longer.

- As with in a sitting meditation, your mind will wander around many, many times. As soon as you notice this, acknowledge when it and return to feel the next step. It's like training a puppy, keep bringing it back.

- Whether your attention was distracted for one second or for ten minutes, simply acknowledge where it was, and come back to being here and now with the next step you take. Be kind to yourself.

- To end, experience yourself standing. Notice the stillness.

- Bring your attention on what is keeping you upright. Feel your body's weight as it sinks down your legs through the soles of your feet into the earth.

- Simply stand, and experience yourself and, with a deep breath, bring this walking meditation session to a close.

MEDITATION USING THE SENSE OF SIGHT

You can meditate using your sense of sight, either with the instrument of sight, your eye, or the subtle sense of sight, something you see in your mind's eye or imagination. You can are visualize an image or a symbol with your mind's eye, the sun, a star, a candle flame, a crescent, a cross, symbol of Om, a lotus flower, your personal deity, etc. Or, you could have a physical point of focus such as the tip of your nose, the pulsation in any particular part of the body, or an image in front of you such as a candle flame, a mandala, a yantra, or sacred image or icon.

There's an ancient practiced called *Trataka,* or Yogic gazing – which uses the sense of sight – both internally and externally. It involves alternately gazing at an object or point without blinking, then closing your eyes and visualizing it in your mind's eye. It increases focus and attention, and creates a sense of deep silence and rest. It's commonly performed with a candle flame but some people choose to gaze at a symbol such as a yantra or a mandala (geometrical diagrams), or at an image of a saint. You can gaze at a flower or a tree, or a cloud, or at night the moon or a bright star can be your focus. You can even gaze into your own eyes into a mirror or someone else's (as they do it with you). Choose one point and stick with it for the practice.

I find the most popular and effective practice is to gaze at a candle flame – it gives you the best after-image when eyes are closed.

MEDITATION USING THE SENSE OF SOUND

Some people use sounds as a focus of their meditation. Some say or sing a prayer or a chant, others listen to sounds such as those found in nature such as the wind in the trees, or the waves crashing on the shore, others listen to chants or bells or crystal bowls. Some listen to subtle sounds in their own body, such as the sound of the breath or the sound of their heartbeat. Others listen to sounds in their mind as they read and reflect on words that inspire them, or sounds they silently repeat as in a mantra or Centering Prayer.

The best known and most widely practiced example of sound-focused meditation is Contemplative prayer. Spoken and written prayers are found in most faith traditions. As you read spiritual, sacred and inspiring texts silently or aloud, you deeply reflect on the meaning. Listening to sacred music, spoken words or any music you find relaxing or inspiring is also a way to reflect using the sense of sound.

The meditation practices and exercises you'll learn in this program that focus on the sense of 'sound' are:

- Self–Inquiry & Heart's Desire Practice
- Silent Mantra Meditation

Self-Inquiry

There was a wise man from south India, Ramana Maharshi, whose followers would ask him all sorts of spiritual questions. He often responded to questioners with another question, such as, "From where did that thought arise?" or "Who is thinking the thought?" He found these questions helped to quiet the mind and to inquire into one's true nature. He also taught his followers to ask the question, "Who am I?" The fact that you can question yourself and your thoughts means there is a thinker of the thoughts: the one who is experiencing the thoughts. By simply asking the question you connect with this aspect of yourself, your soul.

This practice has you ask yourself that same question, and a few others, before you proceed with your sitting meditation. It's a practice of simply asking a question, be present with the question itself, and listening. You learn to trust that the answer will meet the question, at some point in time, in or out of meditation.

Read through the following instructions. Do this practice for a fixed period of time as you would a sitting meditation, it's suggested to do this technique for 10-20 minutes. You can do it by itself, or after or before a Silent Mantra Meditation or Breath Awareness Meditation.

Here's how:

- Sit comfortably. Let your body settle and relax. Keep your eyes closed or capped.

- Practice the heart-centered breath for a few minutes.

- Now, let your breath be soft and natural.

- Ask yourself this question silently: *Who am I?* Don't answer the question with your mind; instead, ask, wait, and listen.

- Be comfortable with the silence and the unanswered question.

- You might hear an answer right away, you might not hear anything at all, or you might feel something. Let go of expectations and be present with the question for a few minutes.

- Ask yourself again. *Who am I?*

- Don't make up an answer. Instead, maintain a beginner's mind. No expectations.

- The answer might meet your question now, later today, a week from now, or in a month. The answer might come in meditation or in activity.

- Let that question go, and then ask a new question: *What is my heart's desire?* Do the practice as before.

- Then, after a few minutes, let that question go, and any answers you may have heard, and ask: *How can I best love myself?*

- The most important part of this exercise is to ask the question, not to make up any answers to it.

- After you sit in silence for a few minutes, let go of the questions and any answers you might have heard. If you continue with your sitting meditation practice, do so without further thought of the questions.

Silent Mantra Meditation

Mantras used in meditation are found in every culture and religion. The word *mantra* comes from the combination of two syllables: "man," meaning "mind" or "awareness," and "tra", meaning "tool for" or "agent of." I find mantra meditation very effective. I use a mantra for its vibrational quality, not its meaning.

A mantra is a sound, word, or phrase that is repeated over and over, either aloud as a chant, or silently. This sound is a point on which to focus your mind, eventually interrupting the constant flow of thoughts (which you hear internally). Over time, this practice trains the mind to settle down to deeper and deeper levels of thought, allowing you to transcend, or go beyond, your world of form and phenomenon and into the world of silence.

Religious mantras include the Lord's Prayer in the Christian tradition, the name of God in Judaism or the Muslim religion, the *Om Mane Padme Hum* mantra of Tibetan Buddhism, or the Christian mantra *Maranatha* in ancient Aramaic meaning "Come, O Lord." Some use the phrase *Ma Om.* Some people repeat the name of a saint, or a quality they wish to enliven in life, or a solemn phrase. Examples of these are, *Shalom*, *Thy will be done*, *Peace*, or *All is well*.

Many mantra meditations use Sanskrit syllables, words or a phrase which, when repeated, help to focus the mind. These syllables are sometimes called *bija* sounds. Bija means seed. The most common are *Om*, or *Hum* which are said to have no particular meaning but reflect the sounds of nature. Some people use a mantra and coordinated with their breath. You can even repeat the word *One* as you focus on your breath, as Dr. Herbert Benson write about in his *Relaxation Response*. Some people count their breaths using the numbers one through ten.

The mantra you'll learn is **Ham Sah.** Pronounced "hum sah" (the *m* is soft, almost like the sound *ng.*) This mantra is loosely translated as, "I am that" and has been used for thousands of years. Another version is **So Hum,** and both are linguistic representations of the subtlest sounds of the breath. When you use these mantras or any of the mantras, focus on the sound of the word rather than the meaning of the word.

Read through the following instructions. Review them again each day before you practice. It's natural not to remember each and every step, but as time goes by it will become second nature. Practice this Mantra Meditation each day, twice a day for 5-30 minutes.

Here's how:

- Turn off music, sounds, TVs, what have you.

- Determine how long you'll be doing this practice before you start. Keep track of the time by looking at a clock or watch. Don't set an alarm that will make you get up to shut it off.

- Sit comfortably. Your eyes can be open, half-closed, or closed. The idea is to be still but shift as you need to find comfort.

- Remember to let go of expectations, be kind to yourself, complete the entire practice period, and don't give up.

- Notice the different sounds that become apparent to you.

- Feel your body as you sit still. Scan it to relax and be settled as you learned in the Body Awareness practice.

- Breathe naturally through your nose. Notice the movement of the breath in the body. Do not control or regulate the breath, simply feel its sensations. Do this for a few minutes as you did in the Breath Awareness Meditation.

- After a few minutes on an inhale, think the sound "*hum*", and as you exhale, the sound, "*sah*." (if you prefer a different sound or mantra, adapt these instructions for that practice.)

- Keep your focus on the sensation of your breath while silently repeating the mantra.

- On your next inhalation, gently draw your breath along the back of your throat listening for the sound of "*hum*" in your actual breath.

- As you exhale, listen for the sound of "*sah*" as your breath is amplified in the throat.

- Let your mind become absorbed in the sound of "*hum sah*" in your internal chanting and the sound and the sensation of your actual breath.

- There's nothing to figure out, no particular feeling you should feel.

- Whenever you notice your attention has drifted away from your breath and the mantra to a sound in the environment, a sensation in your body, or a thought in your mind, gently refocus to the mantra.

- It doesn't matter how many times you lose the mantra and have thoughts, see colors, feel emotions or physical sensations. It could be very frequently. Thoughts have nothing to do with how deep you are going or if you are doing it right.

- Do not push away or control anything, simply refocus your attention once you realize it. There is no need to force or concentrate. Be kind to yourself.

- As you sit, all kinds of thoughts will arise. They come and go every few seconds. Thoughts can be in words, such as thinking about desires, goals and every day activities. Thoughts can be visual too; you see them in your mind's eye. They can be memories, colors, shapes, faces, and places. Don't try to stop the thoughts. When you notice your attention has been carried away by them, gently reintroduce the mantra with your breath again, and allow the mantra to again become predominant. This is the training.

- If you notice thoughts along with the mantra, favor the sound of the mantra.

- Continue meditating this way for the entire period.

- When the period ends, allow a few minutes for integration. These means to keep your eyes closed, stop saying the mantra, and sit easily for at least 1-2 minutes for the Integration Period.

- It is very important to take time before jumping back into activity. Don't get up and make sudden movements. During this time, you can gently stretch your body or say a prayer or affirmation, or just bathe in the silence of your own being.

- After a few minutes, slowly open your eyes.

- It's important not to pay attention to the mantra outside of meditation. It is to be used only during meditation. When it comes to mind outside of meditation simply return your attention to what you are doing.

Meditation & Desires

Ancient texts say *you are what your deep driving desire is*. This means your desires when you are on a spiritual path aren't random or accidental. Instead, your desires flow through you on purpose; you desire them because they are meant to be experienced, or to lead you somewhere or to something, to the real you and your potential. What you want is often unique to you. It's not selfish to ask yourself what you want, or to know what you want, or to want what you want. Desires are natural.

Once you do get some clarity about what you want, it's important to let go of how and when what you want is going to manifest. It's also essential to let go of attachment to the desire.

Keep your desires in your heart and have faith. Allow them to be, yet let the universe handle how your desires will manifest. The same intelligence behind the creation of a tree, a flower, a human, a mountain, is what will be activated. The infinite organizing power will conspire to create your desires, in its own way and time you can trust all will unfold perfectly. Don't keep your attention in the future. The future is only an idea, and is truly experienced and created in the present moment.

Your job is to attend to the present moment, accept the present moment as it is - both in and out of meditation. Through meditation, you can more easily dwell in the present moment, this moment right now, and now, and this one too. This is important as it's in the present that you'll realize the next step to take and next choice to make, as well as experience the manifestation of your desires.

Go into meditation. Put your attention on your desires **before or after** your meditation. Then let them go, and begin your practice. If you pay attention to your desires once you begin your breath or mantra meditation, it can interfere with the natural process of the mind settling down.

Experiences in Meditation

It's good to know there are no experiences considered 'bad' in meditation.

You'll definitely like some experience in meditation more than others, but no matter what your experiences are in meditation don't worry about doing it "right." Meditation experiences will be different depending on your ever-changing physical and emotional state and life circumstances. This can include how you slept, what you ate, what your personal interactions were like that day, etc. Don't be surprised when your experiences change but realize that in each meditation you are having the most nourishing experience for you.

You might begin to expect or want your meditation to go a certain way based on previous ones, and this could frustrate you if you don't have those experiences every time. Don't try to repeat your favorite experiences. Instead, treat each meditation with the beginner's mind with no preconceptions as to what will happen. The goal of meditation is not to have special or mystical experiences. It is to simply do it. The practice itself, no matter what the content of it seems to be, will help you to have a better life. By meditating regularly, meditation will become easier, and your body will get used to it.

There is no right or wrong way to feel while meditating.

Sometimes you will feel like you could meditate all day, and other times you'll want to quit. Also, all kinds of emotions will arise in meditation. Some of these you'll like and others you won't. Your job in meditation is to feel what arises, the actual sensations and emotions, and let them pass through you. Also, when you notice you're no longer feeling the feelings but are instead seeking the reasons for the emotion or contemplating the source of the emotion, that's when you return to the focus of your meditation.

A meditation practice can be like brushing your teeth. You do it every day. It's part of your routine. Some days brushing your teeth feels really good, almost satisfying, and other days, you just want to get it over with. It's the same with a meditation practice. However, no matter what your experience is during meditation, you will experience immediate benefits. Whether you 'got to that peaceful place' or not, the benefits of meditation will show up in your life.

Don't try too hard to meditate.

The only thing you can do wrong when meditating is to try too hard to achieve a certain experience, beat yourself up, or try to do it "right." Although meditation can be a way to experience inner silence, this comes about not by trying too hard to stop thinking or eliminating your thoughts – but by going beyond, or transcending the thoughts.

When you sit to meditate you'll probably become more aware of sounds both in your environment and in your head. The sounds in mind are words we think, or thoughts which are linguistically structured. You hear your thoughts such as desires, goals and every day activities. Prayers are thoughts too. Thoughts can also be visual, you see them in your mind's eye. They can be memories, colors, shapes, faces, and places. The nature of the mind is to think, just like the eyes are designed to see and the ears to hear. Don't expect your senses to do anything other than what they are designed to do. When you interrupt the thought with a mantra, a word you think that has little or no meaning, the mind begins to settle down, naturally.

Don't try too hard, try to stop thoughts, or to use effort to meditate. Don't try to think your way to the deep silence either. Forget the 'no pain, no gain' idea. Instead, simply keep refocusing gently and easily on the focus of your meditation. Have faith and be kind and patient with yourself. You can't do it wrong. The most important thing is to just do it.

If you are using a mantra, focus on the *sound* of the sound you are thinking.

Mantras are used for their sound quality. When using the mantra – focus not on the meaning of the word (or anything it reminds you of.) Instead, focus on the vibration, or the sound of the word. This practice works because the mantra interrupts the constant flow of thoughts – which are usually words strung together in your mind, or images in your mind's eye – because the mantra is a word with no meaning. With repetition of the mantra, your mind has an opportunity to settle down and you are more aware of subtler levels of the thinking process. This is natural. The mantra is only to be used in meditation. If you notice the mantra starts to come into your awareness as you are in activity, then favor the activity over the mantra.

Don't force out thoughts or resist them.

Thoughts arise spontaneously in meditation. Remember it is the nature of the mind to think. The thoughts are often a narrative of what is happening in your life, or what is happening in meditation, or what has happened or what will happen. This is a natural part of meditation. Once you become aware that you are focused on a train of thought, simply return your attention to the focus of your meditation. The moment when you realize you aren't focused on your meditation is what I call the *Choice Point* – it's a moment when you make a choice to either come back to the focus of your meditation or continue your daydream. I suggest you be sweet and refocus. With refocusing, you'll train your brain to be more one-pointed. If you have a thought that you feel is important, it will be there when you come out of meditation. However, most thoughts are mundane and will be forgotten afterwards.

It doesn't matter how many times you have to refocus your attention.

You have not made a mistake if your thoughts come over and over again or your attention becomes distracted by a daydream, colors, thoughts or ideas. It's a natural part of meditation. Thoughts in meditation are a good thing, even if they are frustrating because you want it to be some other way.

Meditation is called the ideal antidote to stress because stress is released in many ways during meditation. In meditation, the mind settles down and the body settles down, and balance is recovered. The body and mind purify anything that gets in the way of the optimal functioning and mind body connection. As the body settles down, the mind settles down, and the stress begins to be released.

Stress comes from a variety of sources, mental activity, emotional experiences, environmental influences and physical issues. Stress is also caused by not saying what you mean, or being who you are, or fully experiencing your life in the present moment. All stressors, including experiences you didn't fully 'digest', leave a subtle residue in the body. This is what begins to accumulate in your nervous system.

When you meditate, stress begins to be released, and it moves to be eliminated. This movement of stress being eliminated can create a correlating movement in the mind, body and emotions. Some people experience mental activity when stress is released, such as stimulating thoughts, colors, and ideas. Others experience movement or sensations in the body, such as twitching, pain, heat or coolness, or leaning. Other experience can include emotional releases such as crying, smiling, or fleeting sensations of anxiety or anger.

Thoughts in meditation.

Thoughts in life come and go every few seconds. Thoughts can be in words, such as thinking about memories, desires, goals and everyday activities. Prayers are thoughts too. Thoughts can also be visual, you see colors, shapes, faces, and places in your mind's eye.

Thoughts in meditation are often an indication that you are releasing stress. As the stress stored in your body and energy system begins to be released, this can stimulate a correlating activity in the mind and body. Thoughts are an example of that. It's good to know that thoughts in meditation are often an *indication* of stress being released. It's also important to note that it's the *movement of the thoughts* that indicates stress is being released. The *content of your thoughts* often hasn't anything to do with the source of the stress being released. For instance, you might be thinking of a work issue during meditation, but you could be releasing some environmental stress or stress from an experience that was traumatic long ago.

Thoughts in meditation can also include seeing a variety of colors. This also relates to the release of stress in the energy system of your body. When you see colors in meditation, it's often an indication that stress is releasing in certain areas of the body, allowing energy and information to flow freely. This creates an enhanced healing response and mind body connection. It's good to remember that you don't want to look for experiences in meditation, but instead, want to return your attention back to the focus of your meditation.

Don't stop meditating just because you are restless. Keep your time commitment.

Subjectively it might not feel like you are having a deep meditation, but with objective measures you'd discover you are deeply resting – you'd see this if you were hooked up to an EEG machine, or your blood pressure and respiration rate were monitored. The reality is that your body can be deeply resting even if your mind doesn't think it's true.

When your mind is active, your body may feel restless. This experience may occur at the beginning of a meditation or if you've recently been engaged in emotionally charged or mentally intense activities. You can also feel restless if you've just eaten or done some traveling. Restlessness also means you are releasing stress. As the stress is being released, there is a correlating movement, either in the mind or body. It could look like coughing, twitching, not being comfortable, pain, emotions, etc. This is a good thing.

Stick with your time commitment no matter how restless you are until the time period is up. Keep coming back to your focus as soon as you realize your attention has drifted away from it, even if it you have to do this over and over again. As you continue your meditation during this restless period, you will eventually reduce the stress and the mind will settle down and the body will relax. You may even get the meditator's high after the stress is released. Either way, you'll definitely feel better when you've completed the meditation.

Strong physical responses are a good thing too.

If you notice strong physical activity in meditation such as movement, pain, heat, tingling, or even coughing or twitching, this indicates that your body is releasing stress. Unlike linguistically-structured thoughts in meditation where there isn't a correlation between the content of the thought and the source of the stress itself, the opposite is true regarding physical release. When you experience a physical release, often the stress is being released from that area of the body. If there is movement or a change in temperature, this often indicates a shift in the subtle aspect of the body such as the energy system or the hormones.

When there is a physical sensation in meditation you have two choices: the first is to bring your attention to the sensation relating to the physical release, notice how your body feels and stay with it. If you begin to have thoughts about the area, trying to change your experience, or trying to figure out why you're feeling what you are feeling, then go back to the focus of your meditation. Your other choice is to directly refocus back to the breath or mantra.

Strong emotions indicate the release of an 'undigested' experience.

Emotions are simply the body's intelligence in response to a thought. Some people say emotions are *energy in motion*. If you are uncomfortable with a particular emotion, such as sadness, anger or grief, the tendency may be to want to ignore it when it arises in your everyday life. . If you resist that natural flow or movement, and don't fully experience emotion as they arise, the energy of the emotion becomes "stuck."

When the mind settles down in meditation, strong emotions can arise. It could be that the deep relaxation that meditation creates causes a kind of "unwinding" or purification of an emotion that has been "under the surface." When you feel one come up, allow yourself to experience it fully so the energy of the emotion can flow and restore the body's intelligence.

Emotions in meditation: don't resist them; they usually don't stay too long.

When you feel an emotion in meditation such as fear, bliss, sadness, anger, anxiety, love, etc., it is usually in a pure state. This means the emotions arise without an associate thought and the reasons for them are usually hard to distinguish. However when you feel a strong emotion, it can be a mental habit to interpret why it arises or dramatize it with a story about it.

If anger arises, for example, you might immediately try to figure out what happened in the past that made you so mad, or imagine something happening now as the cause of the anger, such as too much noise in the room, etc. This can intensify or feed the emotion, and it can obstruct the emotion from easily moving through your nervous system. So it is advised not to give the emotion a story, simply feel the sensation. Often, the story isn't even true. When you become aware that you're once again caught up in a train of thought or a story about this or that emotion, simply refocus once again.

If the emotion or thought is so strong that you can't easily refocus, then let your awareness locate a physical sensation in the body that is associated with the strong emotion (or thought). Keep your attention there and the awareness of the sensation will eventually dissolve. You will release the stress, and the mind will be free to continue with the focus of the meditation.

Everyone falls asleep in meditation once in a while.

Sometimes new meditators have the experience of their head bobbing up and down in the meditation. It may feel as if they are falling asleep, but they probably aren't, though it can feel that way (see below: *Transcendence*). That's because meditation takes them into a state of deep relaxation, and they've probably never been at that level of relaxation while still being "awake". I call this the new meditator's nod, and it should stop after a week or two. If you fall asleep during meditation, it simply means your body has accumulated fatigue and is taking the opportunity of your relaxation in meditation to rest. If you haven't already experienced this, you will. Meditation will always give you the most evolutionary purifying and experience. If it happens often, consider going to bed earlier. Another way to be more alert during meditation is to lie down before your meditation period for about 10 minutes. Then sit up to meditate. If you do fall asleep in your meditation, when you wake up, continue your meditation for the duration of the time, or at least for another five minutes.

Noise and interruptions.

It's enjoyable to meditate in a quiet place, but it is not always possible. If you hear noises, don't try to ignore the noise or to block them out. Instead, welcome them, and then simply return the focus onto the breath and/or mantra. It's all a part of meditation - the noise, your thoughts about it, the way the mind may start to resist them, the emotions that arise about it.

Though it is very important to come out of meditation slowly, sometimes you can't do that. You might be suddenly interrupted by an external influence. This can cause a lot of challenges. In meditation your parasympathetic nervous system is dominant – the rest and digest response. Also in meditation you can experience a different state of consciousness, a state that is as deeply restful as deep sleep.

If you get interrupted in meditation, there is an abrupt transition and this sends a shock to your brain. Your body/mind moves from the rest and digest response to the activation of the fight or flight response. And this sudden activation can be very jarring. It's like being deeply asleep and had to jump up to attend to an appointment feeling like you were late. This can really disrupt your inner peace and can wreck your whole day, causing a headache or irritability, or not feeling like yourself. That's why if you do get interrupted in the middle of your meditation, it's ideal go back and meditate for at least five more minutes to release any stress that was created, as soon as you can. And definitely finish your meditation period with a few minutes of sitting still.

If you are unable to go back to meditation, the process in the deep relaxation of meditation of the stress release of the emotions or stress under the surface is interrupted. This can make you uncomfortable all day, until you are able to get back into your meditation.

How does meditation take you to the deep stillness?

When you repeat the mantra effortlessly, and simply 'listen' to it, it gives a busy mind something to focus on. With your focus on the vibration or sound of the mantra, the meaningful association of thoughts and words are interrupted. This interruption disengages the habit of the mind and its activity where one word and its meaning lead to another. You'll soon experience subtler and subtler levels of thought until you transcend thought activity completely. You'll become deeply relaxed, unaware of the mantra or thoughts, unaware of time passing, and your breath seems like it stops. This can feel a little like being asleep. However, unlike sleep you'll be completely awake...... this is the experience of transcending – some call it slipping into the gap.

Transcendence.

When you slip into the gap, you are aware of nothing, no "thing". Your awareness has transcended time and space, you've gone beyond the world of thinking, and are having the direct experience of the source of your thought – the real you – pure awareness, or what some call your soul. You also transcend your self-image and get a sense of your true being. You experience of the field of pure awareness and become aware of awareness itself. It is a very real and powerful experience. Sometimes it lasts only a second or two, for others, it lasts minutes. It can happen so quickly and subtly that you may not realize it. However, as you go in and out of this state, you'll eventually become more familiar with the silence that is naturally present in the mind along with the thoughts.

The field of pure awareness is subtle and intangible. I like to compare it to gravity or magnetism. Gravity is subtle, with no real dimension, but obviously powerful. Electricity is too. You can't point to either of them or sense them in their pure form, but you can experience the effects of gravity and magnetism. The same is true of pure awareness – it's not a sensory experience and you won't know you are diving into it until you come out of it. However, you can experience the effects. Because the soul has no dimension, you won't 'experience' it as you would things with dimension in time and space, but you commune with it. You might notice you feel good and hope the sensation lasts a while, but when you have that thought you are no longer "there" as thoughts are in the relative world of time and space.

Experience an expanded state of awareness.

Each of us lives between three states of consciousness: waking, dreaming, and sleeping. Each of these states has differentiated physiological markers (respiration rates, blood pressure, and brain activity, etc.) and differentiated levels of awareness (dull, active, alert).

In the waking state (where you probably are now) you are alert and there are thoughts, feelings, and images that you are aware of. In dreams you have some thoughts, experiences, and emotions and your mind is active, though you might not be very alert. In deep sleep state you do not have any emotions, thoughts, or images and you are disconnected from your senses, environment, and experiences. You're in a dull state of awareness, yet you are still alive and fine.

You begin meditation in the waking state and as you go in and out of the transcendent experience, or the gap this is another state of consciousness. It is often described as a dream-like state, somewhere between being asleep and awake. For a brief moment you transcend space and time, you are not repeating the mantra, and there is not a lot of mental activity, you are not aware of the environment, body or breath. Instead, you are directly experiencing awareness itself- not awareness of anything in particular.

This experience is probably new to you. It's actually considered to be an experience of another state of consciousness. In Sanskrit it's called *Atma Darshan*, which means directly experiencing your own soul. This transcendent state of awareness in meditation is a natural experience, just a sleeping and dreaming are; and although it may seem a little dream-like, it isn't a dream at all. It is the experience of being. You can't will this connection or transcendence into happening; it is a natural result of the effortlessness of the meditation process.

Sometimes transcending in meditation feels a little like sleep.

Sleep is the main way your body releases stress as it recovers, restores and recharges. Your blood pressure decreases, your respiration rate slows down, your hormones normalize, cellular repair begins, and your brain dumps excess information and organizes the rest like a computer's defragmenter.

Just before sleep, there is a floating between "awake" and "asleep". This is the time your brain produces Theta waves, and sometimes Delta brain waves. Theta waves indicate that the mind and body are accessing a deep rest. Theta waves are often the same waves produced during meditation. Before you fall asleep, this period lasts only a few minutes. When you meditate you can almost immediately "land" in this deep rested state and extend it for a while. It is the experience of this state that enlightens you to a world beyond your senses. It is said that an extended period in this state makes one more receptive to intuition and the perfection of life.

How Meditation Works

It is said that people have tens of thousands of thoughts a day.

Thoughts come and go every few seconds. From the moment you wake up they begin, and they go on and on until you fall asleep. They're still there as you dream. Why does this happen? It's the nature of the mind to think. Because most of us think in words, and words have meaning, it stimulates another thought. No wonder that when people want to meditate, and they sit still and close their eyes, they immediately get frustrated because the thoughts that have always been there come to the forefront of their awareness. They then try to stop them. You must know this: it's impossible for 'you' to stop them. You cannot stop thinking by thinking about it. However, if you meditate and stick to the meditation procedure you have been taught, the thoughts and the thinking process can be interrupted and eventually settle down. It does require a little faith in the practice and a bit of patience.

Training the brain.

Although meditation can be a way to experience inner silence, this comes about not by eliminating thoughts, but by interrupting the thinking process. When you meditate using a focus (either the sound or sensation of your breath, a mantra, or a visual focus) you can refocus again and again and interrupt the constant flow of thoughts, reactions, and distractions that you have. This will help you to experience subtler levels of your mental activity. The process of thought might even seem to stop for a time.

This is a natural process and happens by itself over time, if you commit to practicing regularly. When your thoughts settle down, you eventually experience the silence and peace that is the backdrop of the thoughts. Seasoned meditators say that all they have to do is have the intention to meditate, shut their eyes, and they are in the silence, immediately.

With regular practice you'll become more aware of your awareness.

Contrary to popular belief, you can't think your way into that peaceful place. Instead, you have to do a practice that naturally helps you to settle down and go beyond, or transcend thought and mental activity. You are not your thoughts, but you become more aware of them in meditation. But who is the one thinking these thoughts? As you meditate, you begin to identify more with the *thinker of the thought* rather than the thoughts themselves. You become more aware of your own pure awareness with its qualities of stillness, peace, receptivity, love, contentment, and pure energy.

The big shift.

This inner stillness becomes your reference point as you engage in life, eventually replacing the reference point most of us use to determine how we feel or who we are - the world out there and our roles and responsibilities in it. It's a subtle yet powerful shift in perspective – a new normal – because instead of rushing around and being unstable and frazzled due to life and the circumstances you face, you become more centered within. You are constantly connected to and accessing a center point of stillness that is stable, steady, and independent of the ever-changing world "out there." I call this being *soul-centered.*

Meditation is the tool that you use to become more intimate with the real you, and directly experience your own awareness. The real you is just that – awareness – that part of you that has been with you since you can remember. The scenery – the body, the experiences, the relationships – change, but the real you, sometimes called your soul, is the 'one' that you become more intimate with through meditation. It is the part of you doesn't change.

As you meditate, your attention naturally shifts from the objects of perception, or your environment or thoughts themselves, to the one who is having of the thoughts, to you, the experiencer. You begin to relate, or refer, more to this part of you. You'll be in activity and the awareness of your being will be more present at all times. Your center point of peace will become more stable. You'll begin to experience a more settled, peaceful mind, and so when faced with a choice, you'll naturally make more nourishing ones.

When you meditate regularly, the benefits will become evident over time.

Each meditation is exactly what your body and mind need for rejuvenation and stress reduction. In addition to the myriad of mind and body health benefits, meditation can increase intuition, helps you to make better choices, makes you feel more peaceful, and some people notice more 'coincidences' or synchronicities occurring in their lives. You don't have to pretend you are now spiritual or enlightened. Mystic visions, discovering your past lives, and ESP can be very alluring, though unlikely in these practices. And though some meditators report some of these experiences, they definitely shouldn't be the goal. Meditation can help you to get clearer about who you really are and what you really want. The true purpose of meditation is to have a better life.

Fight or Flight to Rest and Digest

Anytime you encounter a threat to your safety a cascade of physical and emotional reactions is provoked. This stress response is known as "fight or flight" response. It arises from a primitive part of the brain and is designed to ensure our survival.

Physiological changes that happen as a result of the fight or flight response are:

- Heart rate and blood pressure increase to increase flow of blood to muscles

- Breath rate increases to oxygenate body

- Stress hormones are released – cortisol, glucagon, and adrenaline

- Circulation of blood is shunted away from digestion and sex organs toward heart and lung to increase oxygenation and its delivery to muscles

- Body starts to sweat

- Stickier platelets (blood clotting cells) in case of injury

- Immunity changes focus to immediate surrounding threats

If a challenge before you is life threatening, these bodily changes are useful. The way the body *normally* discharges these excess hormones is through running, exercising or moving. *Or fighting and fleeing.*

But if the threat is psychological (like a fight with our spouse, or difficult issues at work) rather than physical, this unnecessary activation of the fight or flight response weakens your mental and physical health. Unfortunately, most of us are triggered into the fight or flight response without any physical threat and this routine unnecessary activation of hormones and changes in the body do us more harm than good.

Most of us can't avoid stressful situations, but we can avoid the long term effects of stress if we are proactive.

Sleep is one of the primary ways the body normalizes the excess stress and balances the stress hormones. It's vital for rejuvenation and purification too. Making time for exercise, creativity, recreation, and being with loved ones can reduce stress too. Taking deep breaths and appreciating life are good first steps for all of us. You can also check the *Peacefinder Exercises* for other ways to reduce stress on the spot.

A regular practice of meditation helps is a great way to create a new normal as you incorporate the restful alertness in your body and mind. Rather than being regularly stressed, meditation can help to create a centered way of being in the world – and like a muscle memory, you will notice you are less reactive and more responsive.

Meditation reduces activity of the sympathetic nervous system responsible for the fight or flight response. Multiple studies show that during meditation the brain and the body chemistry change and the parasympathetic nervous system (the rest and digest response) ensues, creating changes in circulation, immunity, and brain wave patterns. The stress hormone cortisol decreases while the feel good hormones increase. Though very subtle, they can provide a rush of energy and happiness and are much more powerful than narcotics.

Some of the physical changes that occur when you meditate:

- Blood pressure and circulation normalizes
- The heart rate decreases
- Breathing quiets and there is reduced oxygen consumption
- Stress hormones cortisol and lactic acid are reduced
- Sweating is reduced
- Metabolism decreases
- Immunity is strengthened

During meditation you gain a deep rest as in deep sleep, however, you are not sleeping, though your mind is settled, and your body is relaxed. In meditation, instead of being in a dull state of awareness as you are in sleep, you are alert and aware. This is considered a restfully aware state. Perhaps this is why people feel rested after they meditate.

Even a few minutes of meditation every day can help cultivate a sense of balance and vitality that before might have seemed elusive when you were faced with stressful situations. In the morning, a meditation can help you feel more alert and relaxed all day. And, when you get home from work, you can meditate to help you shift gears and transition from work mode to your life at home.

Peacefinder Practices

Meditation is more of a vitamin pill than an aspirin. It's to be used to create an established sense of peace, not to be used to treat a stressful situation when it arises. Besides, it's not always prudent to stop everything you are doing and sit down and meditate. Though meditation can prevent reactivity and the build-up of stress, sometimes you need a quick fix, a prescription for peace, especially if you are feeling trapped in a stressful situation. Here are a few simple practices you can do to find some peace. No one even has to know you're doing them.

Practice each of these exercises below as you read them; each takes less than a minute. You'll have them on hand when you need to refresh your attitude or shift your body's stress response.

- **Close your eyes:** You can usually close your eyes without being noticed, even if just for a half a minute. Try it now. The outside world takes a backseat while you go within. You almost instantly regain a sense of balance and relaxation.

- **Feel your breath:** You can find inner peace with your eyes open, too. Focus your attention on your breath as you slowly take in a deep breath through your nose, then, let it out slowly through your nose. Pause for two seconds, then repeat. Holding the breath after you exhale helps counteract stress patterns of shallow breathing or holding the breath in. In, out, hold, repeat.

- **Count your breaths:** Eyes open or closed, it might help to silently count your breaths. In, count one; out, count two. Count your breaths all the way to ten. The mind might wander, but simply keep bringing your focus back to your breath and counting. This helps calm your nervous system.

- **30-second body scan:** Bring your attention to how your body feels, sitting or standing, right where you are at this moment. With your eyes open or closed, scan your body from the top down, front and back, relaxing as you go. Relax your forehead, your eyes, your mouth, your tongue, your jaw. Lower your shoulders and relax your belly. Bring your attention to your hands, then your feet. In less than a minute, you can feel better from the inside out.

- **Say a prayer or affirmation:** Silently repeating a prayer or an affirmation can immediately shift your focus from a stressful situation to peace. Slowly say a prayer in your mind or repeat an affirmation. *All is well, I'm doing the best I can*, and *This too shall pass* are good examples. You can also choose a single word, like *One, Peace, Trust, or Calm*. Repeat the chosen word or phrase seven times.

- **Slow down:** Do one thing at a time, just a little slower than usual. Get up from your chair more deliberately or walk a bit more slowly—you'll find that this helps ease the tension, brings you back to the present moment, and relaxes your mind and body.

- **Pay attention to each one of your senses:** What are you hearing in this moment? What are you feeling? What are you seeing? What do you taste? What do you smell? By paying attention to your senses, your focus can shift back to the present moment just enough to relieve stress.

- **Smile:** Give yourself a smile (don't grimace.) Smiling releases endorphins that reduce stress and help you feel better. Studies have shown that even faking a smile can lead to feeling happier. Even if it feels strange at first, make it a point to smile more often.

- **Excuse yourself:** If you're unhappy in the moment, or if you're around people who are unhappy, the discomfort can be contagious. Whenever you notice signals of stress in your body, simply excuse yourself, "I've got to get back to a project," and walk away. That project is your inner peace. Go outside, back to your desk, or head to the bathroom. Once there, use one of the above techniques.

A Review of the Simple, Easy, Every Day Meditation™ Method

Remember these **Five Essentials in meditation**:

- It's okay to have thoughts in meditation, they are a natural part of the meditation process.

- Be kind to yourself, no matter what experiences you are having in meditation

- Don't force, concentrate, or try too hard.

- Maintain a beginner's mind – relinquish expectations or anticipation.

- Stick with the practice and complete the length of time you've determined you'll meditate.

The suggested SEED Meditation® Method includes meditating formally for 10 – 30 minutes, twice a day, every day:

- Determine how long you will meditate for, and time it.

- Find a comfortable spot where you'll be undisturbed.

- Sit comfortably, close your eyes, and welcome the moment.

- Start with the Long, Slow, Deep Breath for a few minutes.

- Practice Body Awareness for a few minutes, gradually scanning and relaxing your body from head to toes.

- Practice Breath Awareness for a few minutes, noticing sensations and sound of the breath.

- Introduce the Heart-Centered Breath for a few minutes.

- Practice Self-Inquiry for a few minutes (optional).

- Silent Mantra Meditation for up to 30 minutes.

- When your meditation period is completed, sit or lie down with your eyes closed for at least 2 minutes for the Integration Period.

During the day, you can practice any of these to reduce stress build up:

- mindfulness practices including the Mindful Walking Meditation

- the Long, Slow, Deep Breathing Practice

- the Body Awareness/Relaxation Practice

- turn your attention to your breath as in the Breath Awareness Meditation

- the Heart-Centered Breath practice

- the Self-Inquiry practice

- and the Peacefinder Practices

Remember, meditation works even if you don't think it does. **don't give up.** The benefits of meditation accrue from your very first experience. Don't judge your success by the experiences you have in meditation. Instead, look at how your life is going; are you happier, less stressed, more creative, calmer, more centered, feeling better? You will be!

Part II: Why Should I Meditate?

People turn to meditation for many different reasons. Some are seeking wellness and use it to deal with physical or mental health issues. Others rely upon it to help them get through a transition in their lives, or to deal with difficult emotions, to recover after trauma or tragedy.

It's been adopted by schools to help relieve students' anxiety, by new parents to regain a sense of calm, by corporate executives to reduce stress and make better decisions. Also there are those who use meditation to tap into their creativity or to enhance their sports or work performance.

For a growing number of people, perfectly healthy people, meditation is used as a means of stress reduction and prevention. The reasons to meditate are numerous but I find most people learn to meditate because on some level they are seeking happiness and a more fulfilling life. **People also learn to meditate because they want to:**

- Find that something missing in their life – even though they have everything that they thought they wanted;

- Escape a sense of suffering or emotional pain;

- Feel calmer, relaxed, centered, more balanced, and energized more often;

- Be able think more clearly, focus more easily, and make better decisions;

- Feel more confident and have higher levels of self-esteem, and become more self-aware;

- Find more well-being, enliven their mind-body connection, and create healthier habits;

- Relieve insomnia, depression, or anxiety;

- Activate the healing response or prevent disease;

- Be more attractive or more youthful;

- Find their soul-mate or a nourishing relationship;

- Identify what they really want out of life and clarify their goals;

- Have more access to their innate inspiration and creativity;

- Deeply understand their own and other people's feelings and emotions, and become more compassionate;

- Feel more connected to everyone and everything and savor life more;

- Respond to the calling of their own spirit;

- Listen to their inner knowing and trust themselves more;

- Discover who they really are;

- Find a connection to God or a higher power.

Each of us will experience benefits in different ways. Some people notice dramatic changes immediately, while for others it may take weeks or months. It is not uncommon for other people to notice changes in you before you do.

Meditation evokes a very deep state of physical rest that helps get rid of stress and enhances healing. It normalizes blood pressure, reduces levels of stress hormones, and optimizes the immune system.

Studies also show that meditation brings about increased energy, improved perception, focus, memory, and creativity. Regular meditators have been found to be more compassionate, happier, more relaxed, and more productive than non-meditators. Meditators report a greater sense of inner peace and higher levels of confidence, a clearer mind, and better decision-making. When your mental functioning improves, you feel more balanced and self-aware. Your intuition is enhanced and many say meditation helps them to figure out what they really want and are able to clarify their goals.

The Ideal Antidote to Stress

Almost all of us, if asked, would say that our lives are pretty intense and very busy. There are so many reasons to not sit down and be still. To feel good or worthy, we feel we must be doing something, or accomplishing something, or creating results. This constant doing creates stress.

Are *you* stressed out? Probably. Though it may be obvious to you what causes your stress, there are some sources of stress you may not be aware of. Stress can come from constant or loud noises and air pollution, impure water and food, getting involved in arguments or being around angry people, and continual negative self-talk. Stress can be from having too much to do, and not enough time to do it. It can be from not getting enough sleep, by not eating nourishing foods or digesting food well, or it can arise from simply living out of tune with nature's rhythms.

Just a short time ago in human history, humans were much more connected to nature than we are today. Even as little as 200 years ago, there were fewer artificial sounds and electromagnetic vibrations from telephones, computers, or machinery. There were fewer stresses and diseases resulting from the industrial world. We heard the streams flow, felt the sensation of the breeze across our skin, saw the beauty of the stars in the sky, and enjoyed the scent of the earth. Nature was the absolute governor of our daily and seasonal routines! The natural tempos were easy to follow in every aspect of life: eating, sleeping, working, resting. We woke when it was light, slept when it was dark, and ate locally grown natural foods during daylight. The cycles of nature – night and day, and the planting and harvesting seasons – created an undeniable connection which still exists in some parts of the world today.

Nowadays some of us live our entire lifespan without really ever contacting nature in a direct way. Whether it's being in artificially controlled climates with artificial smells, or eating food from stores or fast food restaurants that had been packaged in a far-off factory a long time ago, then zapping it in a microwave; we are gradually divorcing from our natural origins and our organic, original pace of life. This separation causes a lot of stress as our bodies have not evolved quickly enough to handle this new lifestyle.

Stress accumulates in your nervous system often without you even noticing it. It's like dust accumulating on a glass table or mirror. You don't notice it at first, but then soon it's thick enough that you can write your name in it.

The accumulated stress can have an effect on your love of life, your mental health and your physical wellbeing. And stress can lead to a wake-up call. Stress can lead to psychological issues as you continually repeat behaviors towards yourself or the world around you that aren't so nourishing, and lose your creativity and inspiration. Eventually some people sense dissatisfaction or even a depression.

Though you may have been a happy child or teen, stress can accumulate and affect even the joyful, creative and content person you once were. It can make you feel disconnected from life, or as though your choices are limited. It can make you feel as if the world is not a friendly place and life is happening *to you* rather than *for you*. The process is often so subtle; you don't know how it happened or why you feel this way. Resolving the situations that cause stress is vital to emotional and physical health.

A build-up of stress in the nervous system can inhibit the free flow of energy and information, and over time, it can cause or worsen all kinds of physical issues or chronic problems such as high blood pressure, digestive disorders, depression, diabetes, cancer, infertility, insomnia, allergies, and suppress the immune system. Brain nerve cells are worn away by the effects of stress hormones. Stress also affects the immune response and is associated with increased fat around the organs, which is a serious health risk. Your body can begin to age more quickly.

Maybe you realize you are increasingly dependent on medication for your natural bodily functions. It's the way of life today. It's commonplace to take medication normal physical functions for digestion, sleep, having sex, going to the bathroom, breathing, fighting colds. People are dependent on medication to relieve headaches, pain, high blood pressure, depression, anxiety, and allergies. Each one of these disorders are either caused by or made worse by stress. Many people coming to learn meditation are on a whole slew of medications. But here's the problem: medications don't treat the cause, only the symptoms. Let's treat the cause: stress. Meditation can help with that.

Meditation is like a reset button for your mind and body. It brings about balance physically, emotionally, and mentally and gives you spiritual solace. Because the mind and body are intimately connected, when the mind settles down in meditation, so does the body. When this happens, the reduction of stress-induced physical symptoms follows. With a regular practice of meditation you can cultivate this sense of inner peace and balance.

Ways that meditation benefits the body:

Most disease and chronic conditions are caused or worsened by stress, disease itself can increase "stress hormones." Over 80% of all doctors' visits are due to stress-related complaints, and often, stress is due to not being able to create a balance between commitments, activity, rest, recreation, personal relationships, and work. Meditation helps to reduce stress and people 40 years and older **go to the doctor 73% less often** if they have a daily meditation practice. Meditators also have over 85% fewer hospital admissions for heart disease and over 55% fewer admissions for all types of benign and malignant tumors.

One of the biggest benefits from meditation is the **general calming of the nervous system,** lowered heart rate, and lowered blood pressure. Harvard Medical School reported that those who face borderline hypertension respond extremely well to meditation, with those under the age of 40 expecting to fall below the limit set for borderline hypertension, which is about 130.

Not only does meditation lower heart rate and blood pressure, help people quit smoking, and conquer drug and alcohol addictions, it also **regulates hormones**, including reducing cortisol -the stress indicator, and increasing DHEA – the youth hormone.

In 1982 a study was published in the International Journal of Neuroscience, which stated the **biological age** (as measured by blood pressure, and visual and auditory performance) of long-term meditators was significantly lower than those with their same chronological age. Long-term meditators who had been practicing a silent meditation technique twice a day for 20 minutes for more than five years were physiologically 12 years younger than their chronological age. Short-term meditators were physiologically 5 years younger than their chronological age.

Another study, which researched elderly meditators, published in 1989 in the Journal of Personality and Social Psychology, reported that people in their 80s showed a marked improvement rather than deterioration in their mental and physical health and well-being over a three year period of practicing meditation. **Benefits for the meditating elderly** included: reversal of aging; increased longevity; increased cognitive flexibility (including increased learning ability and greater perceptual flexibility); increased word fluency; improvements in self-reported measures of behavioral flexibility and aging; greater sense of well-being; improved mental health; and reduction of blood pressure to more ideal levels.

Here are some other proven physical effects that show up with a regular practice of meditation:

- Lowered buildup of plaque in coronary arteries
- Decreased chronic pain
- Reduced stress and fatigue
- Lowered blood pressure
- Reduced insomnia
- Reduced stress on the cardiovascular system
- Reduced symptoms of PMS and menopause
- Reduced doctors' visits and post-operative complications
- Decreased muscle tension and headaches
- Improved circulation
- Balanced blood sugar
- Increased "youth hormone" DHEA
- Increased neuroplasticity

- Improved eating and sleeping habits
- Increased healing response
- Improved digestion
- Increased fertility
- Increased energy and vitality
- Improved sleep
- Improved immune system functioning
- Increased longevity

Meditation is good for the mind too.

Those who meditate report a greater sense of inner peace and wellbeing. They also report higher levels of self-esteem, a clearer mind, the ability to focus on one thing at a time, and to make better decisions. Others say they are less dependent on what others think or say about them to feel good about themselves and have genuine self-acceptance. Many say it helps them to figure out what they really want and clarify their goals.

When different types of meditation are introduced into schools academic performance is improved. It's been shown that meditation helps to reduce test anxiety, nervousness, self-doubt, and concentration loss. Another study funded by the National Institutes of Health showed that students trained in a simple relaxation meditation and sound meditation, showed significant decline in absenteeism, rule-breaking, and suspensions.

A regular practice or meditation will make a difference in social situations too. Fear and anxiety will no longer be constant companions, instead you'll find yourself more calm and centered and this can be good for your relationships. When you're stressed out, it can affect everyone around you at home and at work. It keeps you from being available emotionally for others. People who regularly meditate say they are more engaged emotionally and mentally when they are with their loved ones or doing their work, rather than being distracted and missing the experience of their lives. People also find that meditating together is a deeply peaceful experience.

Here are some other proven psychological effects that show up with a regular practice of meditation:

- Greater sense of calmness, inner peace & wellbeing
- Higher levels of self-esteem
- Increased mental clarity, memory, creativity, & concentration
- Increased attention span & ability to focus on one thing at a time
- Improved decision making skills
- Increased fluid intelligence (IQ)
- Increased self-awareness and self-acceptance
- Improved academic performance
- Improved job satisfaction, performance, efficiency, & productivity
- Improved emotional and mental engagement
- Increased calmness in the face of difficulties
- Enhanced appreciation of life
- Reduced ADHD and ADD symptoms
- Reduced dependency on what others think or say
- Reduced test and performance anxiety
- Decreased nervousness, fear, & anxiety
- Reduced reactivity to stress
- Decreased depression
- Reduced compulsive behavior
- Decreased need for addictive substances

Meditation: It's also good for the soul.

Along with the many psychological and physical benefits, when you practice meditation daily, you benefit spiritually. You'll connect with your true self, that essential part of you that is peaceful and content no matter what is going on outside in your world. You'll also become more aware of who you really are. Your happiness and peace isn't dependent on the roles you play, responsibilities you have, relationships you are in, or the labels you take on. You'll have access to an inner knowing, your internal GPS, some would call your intuition. You can easily tune into your true feelings, including the way your body responds to the situations you face. This helps you to get clearer about what you want and make better choices that are in line with your own integrity. You'll live a self-directed life.

It has also been shown that meditation creates:

- Increased awareness of one's essential self
- Deepened sense of faith
- Increased feeling of safety and being supported by life
- Increased peace, joy, & freedom
- Increased present moment awareness & spiritual awareness
- Enlivened qualities of the heart
- Improved sense of purpose and fulfilment
- Increased compassion toward one's self & others
- Increased feeling of connectedness with life
- Improved access to the power of attention & intention
- Increased intuition
- Increased coincidences & synchronicities

A Few Favorite Studies

I know from my own experience that people's lives can be altered through practicing meditation, and I always am happy when the studies prove it. Take, for instance, the fact that meditation can make you sleep better, enhance your immunity, and it can prevent heart disease and it can reduce chronic pain. It also can change the brain.

In 1996, The American Journal of Medicine reported the results of the study: *Perceived benefits in a behavioral-medicine insomnia program* conducted by Gregg D. Jacobs, PhD, Herbert Benson, MD, and Richard Friedman MD. Over 100 patients with chronic insomnia participated in a daily meditation practice and **each and every patient reported improved sleep at post treatment,** with the majority (58%) reporting significant improvement. Of sleep medication users, 91% either eliminated or reduced medication use. At a 6-month follow-up, 90% of respondents rated improvement in sleep as either maintained or enhanced. This could have a profound effect. About 30-40% of adults say they have some symptoms of insomnia within a given year, and about 10-15% of adults say they have chronic insomnia according to the National Center for Sleep Disorders Research at the National Institutes of Health.

Meditation improves immunity. *Brain, Behavior, & Immunity* in 2008 reported a UCLA study with HIV positive patients which found that after an 8-week meditation training course, patients who'd meditated showed **no decline in lymphocyte content (T-cells, white blood cells important for those with HIV) even while under stress,** compared with non-meditators who showed significant reduction in lymphocytes. Lymphocyte levels went up with each meditation session and the more meditation classes people attended, the higher the T cells.

Researchers Richard Davidson, PhD, Jon Kabat-Zinn, PhD, and their colleagues at the University of Wisconsin **found improvement in the immune system** after 8-weeks of meditation. The study published in 2003, *Alterations in Brain and Immune Function Produced by Mindfulness Meditation*, looked at healthy employees who received the flu vaccine. Those who went through an 8-week meditation training program had significant increases in antibodies to influenza compared with those in the control group.

Meditation produces powerful pain-relieving effects in the brain, according to research findings published in 2011 in the *Journal of Neuroscience*. Researchers at Wake Forest Baptist Medical Center say that they've conducted the first study on pain to show that only a little over an hour of meditation training can dramatically reduce both the experience of pain and pain-related brain activation. Fifteen healthy volunteers attended four, 20-minute classes to learn a breath awareness meditation technique. With an MRI, researchers scanned areas of the brains associated with detecting pain before and after meditation. They found about a **40% reduction in pain intensity and a 57% reduction in pain unpleasantness** after the meditation training. Meditation produced a greater reduction in pain than even morphine or other pain-relieving drugs, which typically reduce pain ratings by about 25%. What's even more exciting is that while participants were meditating during the scans, the activity in the pain-processing region could not even be detected!

A study by Dr. Natalia Morone of the University of Pittsburgh, School of Medicine published in November 2009 showed that **seniors with chronic lower back pain felt better** and were able to function better after 8 weeks of meditation training. This is good news since about 50% of the 37 million seniors alive today live with chronic pain.

In October 2007, *Arthritis & Rheumatism* reported results of a study on adults with rheumatoid arthritis (RA) who were trained in meditation and meditated using sitting meditations, breath awareness, and walking meditations and body relaxations, showed a **35% decrease in emotional distress and a higher quality of well-being** than their counterparts who did not meditate after six months of practice.

Research shows **meditation can change the physical structure and composition of your brain**. In January, 2011, researchers from Massachusetts General Hospital and the Center for Mindfulness at

University of Massachusetts (UMass) Medical School used magnetic resonance imaging (MRI), a kind of super x-ray, to show that meditation can change the brain. This study showed that gray matter in the brain is altered after only 8 weeks of meditation—with those who practiced on average 27 minutes a day – and affecting the part of the brain relating to **peace, compassion (and self-compassion), creativity, connectedness, and awareness of the present-moment**. The changes don't only appear during the practice of meditation, but have a lasting, long-term effect—becoming hardwired into the brain after just 8 weeks.

It doesn't take a scientific study to know that meditators feel less stress, more peace, equanimity, and an enhanced sense of well-being. In fact, these effects have been recorded in the earliest texts on yoga and meditation in India, China, and Japan. Modern day brain imaging, it seems, is now catching up with what ancient wisdom has been saying all along: meditation helps you to live a peaceful life, and your being peaceful helps create a peaceful world.

**"If there is to be peace in the world,
there must be peace in the nations.
If there is to be peace in the nations,
there must be peace in the cities.
If there is to be peace in the cities,
there must be peace between neighbors.
If there is to be peace between neighbors,
there must be peace in the home.
If there is to be peace in the home,
there must be peace in the heart."**

-Lao Tzu, 6th Century BCE

About Sarah McLean

Twenty-five years ago Sarah fell in love with meditation. Ever since, she's explored the world seeking the secrets to meditation. She was a resident in a Zen Buddhist monastery, lived in an ashram in India, taught English to Tibetan Buddhist nuns, bicycled along the silk route through Pakistan, meditated in temples in Thailand and Japan, and trekked the Golden Triangle in Asia. She's also worked with some of the greats in the world of self-awareness – serving as the founding education director of Deepak Chopra's mind-body center for wellbeing, the director of Byron Katie's School for the Work, and assisting Seat of the Soul author, Gary Zukav.

Sarah is passionate about teaching and sharing what she's discovered about how to meditate, and makes it her mission to support those who want to learn how to meditate to find fulfillment, better health, and inner peace. Her best-seller *Soul-Centered: Transform Your Life in 8 Weeks with Meditation* (Hay House) has inspired people everywhere to "take time out for time in" through meditation and mindfulness practices.

She's a speaker at Hay House events, Esalen, Omega Institute, Miraval, Unity Village, and at inspirational gatherings nationwide. She shares her work with corporations, and education and health care institutions. She's been featured in the New York Times, Chicago Tribune, Huffington Post, and on Fox Health News As the founding director of the McLean Meditation Institute (MMI) in Sedona Arizona, she offers meditation classes, weekend retreats, and a teacher certification program.

McLean Meditation
INSTITUTE™

The McLean Meditation Institute for Transformative Meditation Training (MMI) in Sedona, Arizona is one of the leading meditation training companies. Thousands of people have attended their programs including classes in the Simple, Easy, Every Day Meditation Method, and weekend meditation retreats such as the Soul Radiance Retreat™, the Creative Soul™ Writing retreat. Many of the students go on to be teachers, taking the MMI Teacher Certification Program.

MMI was founded in 2006 by best-selling Hay House author Sarah McLean. She is known as the face of contemporary meditation. She once headed up the Chopra Center Education department, spent years in a Zen Buddhist monastery, and has traveled much of the world by bicycle. Visit the McLean Meditation Center, home of MMI, in the heart of Sedona, Arizona at 411 State Route 179, or connect with the Institute online at www.McLeanMeditation.com. (928) 204-0067.

45049277R00049

Made in the USA
San Bernardino, CA
30 January 2017